HANGING BY A THREAD

THE SAVING MOSES JOURNEY

Sarah Bowling

○ ✛ ⓘ

FOREWORD

by Sheila Walsh

I will never forget the first time I stepped inside a malnutrition clinic in Angola, Africa. I had seen documentaries on the impact of hunger and starvation on families and children, the most vulnerable, but nothing prepared me for what I was about to witness.

It was stiflingly hot as we jumped out of the truck and walked toward the narrow brick building. I could hear the sounds of children but they were not the sounds of laughter; they were sounds I'd never heard before, quiet cries of pain and suffering. It took my eyes a few moments to adjust to the lack of adequate lighting and the dirt and dust that hung in the air, but what I saw and heard that day changed me for good. There were eight or nine beds lined up against each side of the room, each with a mother holding her little one, rocking them, giving her child all she had left to give. I asked one of the healthcare workers how old the child in the first bed was. I guessed she was two or three months old. She was two years old. I thought back to my son at two. I never sat down as he was always on the move, but not this little one. It took all the energy she had left to simply breathe. Her hair was patchy and red, one of the signs of severe malnutrition I learned that day. I sat beside the mother and took her hand in mine. She had no words but the look in her eyes spoke volumes from one mother to another. She loved this little girl with a fierce love. She had done all she could do to provide for her but now she sat in this place of despair.

We climbed up an unfinished open cement stairway in Phnom Penh, Cambodia. I gasped as two little ones ran past us up the stairs, precariously close to the edge and a drop of over twenty feet. We were there to meet three girls who were victims of sex trafficking. This abandoned building project was their home. They looked like children themselves, but each night they returned to a seedy club in the city; their only way of providing for their younger siblings. For one, her father was in jail and her mother had run off with a younger man. At fourteen years of age, she was the bread-winner for her three younger siblings. Another girl sat rocking a baby in a make-shift hammock, suspended between two cement posts. Through our translator, I asked who took care of the little one through the night hours when she is gone. She simply shook her head.

The lyrics of a song that my friend, Phil Keaggy, wrote some years ago played on and on in my mind that night as I tried without success to sleep in the comfort of my hotel room.

Who will speak up for the little ones, helpless and half-abandoned?

As I read this book by Sarah Bowling, I realized that I had discovered one of God's most powerful answers. The work of Saving Moses is changing the lives of little ones around the world; the ones who have no voice, those who get lost in the night.

Through my work with Life Outreach International, and similar organizations, I have the holy privilege of being part of God's answer to the suffering in this world, but I want you to know that when it comes to those who have intentionally tuned into the cries of children and refused to walk away, Sarah is a hero to me. She would reject that title quickly, but I know that when this life is over there will be thousands of little legs running toward her, joy-filled faces lifted to say, "Thank you!"

I know you will love this book, but I want more than that for you. I pray that, as you read, you will hear God's call to you to step into the place where the needs of a suffering world and the compassionate heart of God in you, meet. In that place, you know you are exactly where you were born to serve. There is no better life.

INTRODUCTION

Thanks so much for taking this journey with me! You will experience in these pages the successes, uncertainties, heartbreaks and possibilities that Saving Moses has encountered over the course of our short yet intense existence. As you read these stories and feel the victories and heartbreaks, I pray that you will be inspired and encouraged to stretch beyond your daily living, past your natural talents and into the immense impossibilities to which God may be inviting you.

It's important to note that many of the names of babies, toddlers and various individuals have been changed throughout this book to protect their identities. Regardless of the names being changed, the stories are entirely true.

PART 1 - MALNUTRITION

CHAPTER 1 - ABANDONED NEWBORNS

Who abandons newborn babies? How did they arrive in some random field? Was anything with them, like blankets or bottles, when they were discovered? Were they wearing any clothing? What kind of orphanage has a policy that refuses to accept babies? How does a mom get to a place emotionally and mentally where she can desert her twin newborn girls in a field?

Is she sick, disabled, or maybe a drug addict? Where's the dad, or close relatives? Did the mom die in childbirth? Had the newborns received any medical care? When did they last eat? These are questions that flooded my thoughts as I tried to process the strong maternal feelings I was experiencing. And I wasn't coming up with any answers that seemed to make sense.

I was in Ethiopia, in a town very distant from the capital, holding those small and frail newborn twin girls in my arms. I was altogether unraveled. As I held the abandoned newborns close, my raw maternal instincts ramped into overdrive: nurture, protection, feeding, intense focus, outrage because they had been abandoned, bonding concerns and so much more!

Having three young children of my own, I found myself asking and searching for answers to lots of questions about why and how those precious newborn girls had come to arrive in my arms. After some time, I concluded that the "why and how" were not as important or urgent as the "now."

My journey to now, this emotionally charged moment, appeared to be extremely coincidental. Up to that moment, I'd been a Bible teacher in many different contexts: churches, conferences, retreats, TV, interviews, small groups, international ministry events and lots more. These were all very good opportunities, but I had a friend who felt that God wanted to use my life to not only teach the Bible, but to do much more.

As I reflected on my friend's exhortation, I began to have the same feelings in my own heart. Maybe God had more for me to do. So without any explicit direction, I began to explore different opportunities that might agree with what I felt: I looked into providing clean water for developing world countries, initiating feeding programs for hungry people and facilitating outreach experiences for Americans to serve in the developing world, along with many other ideas.

In the middle of this exploring season, I had the privilege of helping to lead a ministry team to the northern part of Ethiopia. Since this was my first trip to Ethiopia, I was mesmerized by the gorgeous and gracious people, regal in stature with gentle eyes and welcoming smiles. And the landscape, spotted with bushes, trees, fields of grass and tent-like homes, felt old with the passage of the humanity who had lived on that soil for many millennia. I learned during that visit that Ethiopia is the birthplace of coffee, so my introduction to the macchiato was a thoroughly delightful discovery that I relish to this day!

One afternoon, I took a jog into the countryside and remembered that Ethiopians are world-renowned for their marathon records, given their slight build and legendary stamina. As I trounced through the terrain, I attracted a gaggle of playful children, laughing and frolicking as they followed me in playful interest. I imagine they were curious to see what this white woman was doing pounding her feet on ground more accustomed to lithe and fleet steps! The land was beautiful, clean, fresh and expansive. I found myself wishing I had the time and endurance to enjoy several more hours getting acquainted with such a magnificent land.

During our week-long visit we did lots of different activities, which included a small medical outreach in a remote Jewish village, a de-worming clinic, college outreach, dramas and a Vacation Bible School at the orphanage where we were staying. It was an amazing time and I enjoyed the diversity of these experiences.

During this time, one of my friends told me about a set of twin newborn girls who had recently arrived at our orphanage. He explained that the orphanage didn't normally take infants because of the extraordinary quantity of care and unique resources that newborns require. They simply did not have the capacity to properly care for them. In this situation, however, the orphanage had made an exception because the newborn girls had nowhere else to go.

The police had already called all the places throughout the town that might be able to help, and every request was turned down. The police finally rang the orphanage to see if they would take in the newborn girls. They explained that if the orphanage didn't take the newborns, they would be forced to return them to the field where they were found because they had no other option.

In our developed country, it's difficult to understand the limited array of options, if any, in the developing world. This is all-the-more accentuated in remote places, far from the resources and connections that are often found in capital cities. In the developing world, there is usually an absence of government programs for their impoverished citizens. And a shortage of non-profit assistance is common among large swaths of the population living at thread-bare subsistence levels, fighting to survive day to day.

So even though I was stunned to learn about those conditions and deficiencies, I was forced to accept that day-to-day reality, which was dreadful. And it was even more appalling when I saw the reality play out in the survival needs of those baby girls precariously living at the orphanage. In a semi-state of shock, the orphanage quickly agreed to accept them and within several hours the baby girls had a safe and stable place to grow, one day at a time. The orphanage named them Sarah and Ruth.

When my friend with whom I was traveling told me about the newborn girls, I, of course, wanted to meet them. When I did, I was entirely unraveled by them. They were very small, frail, helpless and totally vulnerable. As I held them, I couldn't imagine those infants lying abandoned in a field with no care or protection, exposed to the elements and any predatory animal that might come upon them. They had been lying on the ground for who knows how long.

Tears were streaming down my face and I was speechless. I looked deep into their eyes and saw bright life, strength, hope and vitality, even though their little bodies were super light and frail. I remember putting them back into their cribs and pausing at the gravity of what was happening in their very small, new and fresh lives.

Even now as I write this, it is surreal, as if I am reliving those moments. I am overcome by the same emotions and urgency to save as many babies as I can. After walking out of their room, I took a deep breath to try to get my bearings. This was necessary because when I was in their room, it felt to me as if the world had shifted on its axis. I did my best to go along with the rest of my day but those newborns, Sarah and Ruth, were just a sand's membrane below the surface, and my thoughts and feelings about them continued to swirl inside of me.

During any pause in that day, I kept seeing their eyes and thinking of their care, relieved that they were in a safe place but outraged that they had been abandoned. I also began to question the policy of that orphanage, which did not accept babies or toddlers.

When I returned home from that trip, I settled into the normal daily routines and responsibilities of marriage, motherhood and work. All the while, my friend continued to ask me the same questions, "Sarah, what is the purpose of your life? What are the different ways that God could use your life?" As I reflected on these questions, I began to think about the newborns in Ethiopia, Sarah and Ruth, whom I'd met and held. I also did some research on infants, orphanages, infant mortality rates, etc.

I discovered that many international orphanages are not equipped to care for toddlers, babies and newborns because of the huge commitment of resources and care those small lives require. I also found that there are loads of organizations devoted to childhood education, feeding, clean water, medical care and lots more. But there are no organizations that are solely devoted to the urgent needs of toddlers and babies, ages five and younger.

As I thought about this, it struck me that we are most frail and vulnerable at the beginning and end of our lives. If I could help these little people get safely to the age of five with stable care, genuine love, food, protection and medical assistance, they would stand a good chance of growing up with strong bodies, hopeful futures and healthy worldviews. I talked with my husband about these thoughts and asked for his input and feedback. He was very understanding and encouraging. At the same time, I was ardently praying and asking for God's direction.

One morning during my prayer time, I felt like God put a divine download into my brain. Do you remember the scene from the movie *The Matrix* where the main character, Neo, gets plugged into the computer, which downloads into his brain all of the instructions and knowledge on how to fly a helicopter? After the helicopter information, Jiu-Jitsu was downloaded into his brain, along with lots of other skills.

In kind of the same way, I felt like God downloaded into my heart and mind the vision and name for Saving Moses. I'm not saying that I suddenly knew and understood everything about infant mortality, how to change the statistics, etc. What I am saying is that I felt an incredible surge of vision, direction and passion.

In every way that is uncharacteristic of my normal mindset and actions, I did not impulsively jump up and announce this fresh vision and passion. Instead, I took several days to let it percolate in my heart and thoughts. After some time, I picked up the conversation with my husband about what I sensed God saying to me, and he was fully supportive.

I also talked with my friend who had been asking me those difficult questions about my purpose and future. I shared with him how I felt God was directing me. As I look back now, Saving Moses was birthed in my heart from my personal experiences, my convictions and what I believe to be one of God's most important essentials – genuinely loving the least of the least.

The uncompromising mission of Saving Moses is to provide life-saving resources to babies and toddlers five and younger, where the need is most urgent and the care is least available. I am tremendously honored to receive this assignment from God for many different reasons. One of those reasons is that everything in a person's life builds on what happens in the first few years of their existence.

A person's physical, mental, and emotional health, and much more, are largely formulated and established during the first five years of life. Tragically, if a person doesn't receive proper nutrition during those years, their physical, developmental, and intellectual abilities can be severely limited.

For example, I've met ten and twelve-year-old children who didn't receive proper nutrition and food as infants and their cognitive and physical abilities were nowhere near the levels of an average ten or twelve-year-old. And I've also seen eight and ten-year-olds, whose worldview was formed during the ages of 0-5 in brothels and under the beds where their mom earned a living as a sex worker. Their worldview is filled with fear, manipulation, distrust, anger, duplicity and many more ugly things.

So much of our life, perspective, hope and future are shaped during the years of 0-5. I want to be a conduit to express God's very real and tangible love to this extremely vulnerable and formative age group. Hence, the birth of Saving Moses.

LESSONS LEARNED

COMPASSION

For most of us, it is easier to be compassionate when we understand a person's backstory because it gives us a context to appreciate their struggle. However, I have come to the conclusion that compassion is a choice, even more than an education or understanding. I say this because I have watched as people hear about someone else's hardship or plight and still remain unmoved. And I've also met people who choose compassion as their filter as they hear and interact with other people. The outcomes are much different when compassion is involved.

OUTRAGE

What is the raw nerve in you that evokes outrage? I was outraged to learn that most orphanages don't accept children under the age of three. And I was astounded to learn that there were no humanitarian organizations totally devoted to the beginning and formative years of babies and toddlers. I founded Saving Moses as a response to my outrage.

What outrages you? What keeps you excited or astounded? Maybe that is exactly the area you could possibly focus on in order to make a difference. Maybe you have a friend that is telling you that God has something important for you to do. Maybe this book is in your hands to do just that!

CHAPTER 2 - SCULPTING FOR DEFINITION

We all like the final product, the masterpiece, but seldom enjoy the process or the journey it takes to achieve the goal. To this end, I spent countless hours learning to shoot a left-handed layup in basketball, such that today I'm almost equally proficient with both my right and left-handed layups. And if you think about it, great works take an inordinate amount of time, effort, concentration, dedication, mistakes and even failures. Consider these few examples:

The Sistine Chapel - Michelangelo spent more than four years creating this masterpiece

The Sisters of Charity - Mother Teresa lived in India for 15 years before she received God's call to work among the poor in Calcutta, and even after God's call she spent no less than two years in preparation for that ministry, which has continued for more than 60 years

The light bulb – Thomas Edison is credited with trying one thousand different filaments and ideas to create the modern light bulb. When asked by a reporter, "How did it feel to fail 999 times?" Edison replied, "I didn't fail 999 times. I have simply found 999 ways how not to create a light bulb." *[1]*

Even though history overflows with such noteworthy examples, it seems like our modern thinking has become conditioned to the YouTube phenomenon, which often shows that perfection is attainable in a few simple steps. Reality, however, seems to confirm that we need practice, mistakes, persistence, hiccups and incremental progress. And this has been my journey with Saving Moses from the onset.

Having been permanently altered by my time in Ethiopia where I held Sarah and Ruth, I began researching, learning, conversing and more than anything, changing my perspective, and even values, concerning this plight.

If I were to characterize my first two years of this adventure, I would say those years were defined by negative space, helping me to chisel away and define the identity, purpose and goals for Saving Moses. In those two years, I came to appreciate who Saving Moses is not and what Saving Moses doesn't do, and I found this to be extremely helpful and liberating so that Saving Moses could be strategic, deliberate, and highly successful.

In essence, I began this adventure with a block of marble. I had some idea of what was inside, but I lacked a laser-sharp definition. I began to sand down the corners through various travels and experiences. My first adventure was integrated into a trip to China and Cambodia.

In China, I was planning to tour an orphanage and I was eagerly looking forward to the opportunity! I expected to visit lots of babies and toddlers, since I was told that the orphanage was a large, four-story facility with more than 1,200 children, of whom half were under the age of five. During our tour, as I walked around, I noticed that the orphanage

---

[1] https://instituteforleadershipfitness.com/2012/02/learning-from-failure

was extremely quiet, particularly for one that supposedly housed at least 500 babies and toddlers!

Having three children of my own who had been under five years old all at the same time, I was completely amazed at how quiet the children in that orphanage were. The more that we walked around, the more I understood why they were so quiet.

I saw room after room of pristine beds, no less than 30-40 miniature beds or cribs per room. I saw rooms with physical therapy equipment and rooms with miniature tables and chairs, but in the entire facility I saw fewer than six children.

I saw lots of tiny shoes neatly placed in cubbies, clean and beautiful walker toys for babies supposedly learning to walk, and perfectly made beds, neatly arranged and appointed with meticulous precision, maybe even carefully dusted. And I saw some very friendly, clean and smiley workers, but no babies, toddlers or children.

When I asked the Director where all the babies were, he explained that they were on a field trip. I thought about his reply. How do they take hundreds of babies and toddlers on a field trip? For that matter, what kind of a field trip would these babies and toddlers go on? And how would you facilitate the transportation and logistics for such a field trip? The more I thought about that supposed field trip, the more ridiculous it became to me and I concluded that the Director was either lying or stretching a smidgen of truth past any logical explanation.

To this day, I still do not believe that the facility I visited was a functioning orphanage, looking after more than 1,200 children. I believe that the facility was organized and maintained for foreigners to admire the work of the government to care for orphans. I think the whole thing was a scam to get money and I'm still ticked off about that deception!

After this insightful tour, I made a commitment to myself that I would regularly inspect the places where Saving Moses would be working, to ensure that our resources would be effective and used for maximum impact. Because of this practice, we routinely receive the Gold or Platinum Status with the GuideStar charity rating. So I happily chiseled away at a corner of the marble block.

After several days in China, I went on to Cambodia. Thankfully, after what happened in China, my time in Cambodia was better in the sense of connecting with babies and toddlers in real circumstances and daily living. In Cambodia, I started to see some possibilities of who could be in the block of marble, after some more extensive chiseling, sanding and sculpting.

When I first arrived, I visited a beautiful orphanage in rural Cambodia and concluded that while the orphanage was doing great work, it didn't hasten my heart rate because there weren't any babies and toddlers there. It was noteworthy to me that during my visit to the orphanage, I kept asking and looking for babies and toddlers, perhaps instinctively seeking out the essence of the sculpture that I could feel in my heart.

As I kept looking, I visited some moms in a rural village and learned about the birthing standards of traditional mid-wives. My respect for those moms grew exponentially during that visit, after hearing the bone-chilling tales and harrowing accounts that many of them had been through.

Some of the moms told me of birthing their babies on grass mats with a meager supply of water for washing and hygienic upkeep. One mom shared with me the details of her last delivery, where she began to bleed profusely, and her husband borrowed money from neighbors to get her to the hospital in Phnom Penh to save the lives of his wife and newborn. Despite all of these stories and circumstances, I wasn't able to find any immediate opportunities or application for Saving Moses to facilitate healthy delivery programs for moms and newborns.

When I went to Phnom Penh, the capital of Cambodia, I visited an enormous trash dump, looking for babies and toddlers to learn of their urgent survival needs. I was at a trash dump because my friends explained to me that some of the most marginalized individuals and families in Phnom Penh eke out a living by collecting, recycling and living off such vast trash dumps. Those dumps are often multiple acres in size, with trash as far as the eye can see. And many precious little ones live there.

My friends and I entered the dump and began walking on all kinds of refuse: rotting vegetable peels, decomposing meat on chicken bones, broken down packaging and lots of unidentifiable things that I didn't want to think about. The smell arrested me from the onset, and I was hopeful that it would either decrease as we walked deeper into the trash dump, or I'd acclimate and maybe even get desensitized. I had the fleeting hope that the stench wouldn't leech into my clothes or skin - that it was only environmental and not contagious or portable, but unfortunately, that was not the case.

The further I walked into the dump, the more it seemed to exponentially expand, such that I struggled to see the boundaries. But all the while, I kept thinking about my reason for being there, the babies and toddlers who lived in and around all of that trash. I was determined to find those babies and toddlers, by walking along a path of sorts.

True to my normal ready, shoot and aim philosophy, I was walking ahead of everyone, wearing flip flops and trying to keep my feet from getting too dirty from the garbage. I thought the path was pretty solid, but suddenly, I fell into a soupy collage of unknown garbage, sinking up to my thighs in a foul mixture of trash, goo and liquid of various unknown origins.

My friends who were behind me watched in stunned silence and all I could think of was the trash compactor scene in Star Wars where Luke, Leia and Han Solo were stuck in a similar trash goo with an unknown creature swimming around their legs and feet. I had a crazy, panicky feeling that I needed to get myself out of that sinkhole really fast, before something living started to swim around my submerged legs, or worse, began to nibble on my toes!

Looking back, I'm still not exactly sure how I got out without falling in deeper, but I did get out and then attempted to get some of the muck off me. My friends asked if I was alright and offered me some hand sanitizer, which I gratefully used. I may have sanitized my hands, but the dirt and stench still permeated every square inch of me, and it took a few days for the smell to dissipate.

After the dumpster dive, I kept walking. I figured that I'd already acclimated myself quite thoroughly to my surroundings! I was determined to see how the moms, babies and toddlers in that seemingly endless garbage dump lived and discover what challenges they faced every day to stay alive. Surprisingly, I found that several hundred families use that trash dump as their primary means of survival, collecting food scraps and recyclable material to sell. As I walked around their neighborhood, I met a woman who was almost at the end of her pregnancy, and I got just a small glimpse of her daily living in the dump.

She explained that she was about 7-8 months pregnant and that she already had several children. In contrast, she didn't seem anxious or worried like the ladies in the rural village but was more resigned to her living conditions. She seemed hopeless. When I asked about how and where she would deliver her baby, she explained that she didn't have any other option but to deliver her baby in that trash dump. That was astounding to me! It was hard for me to imagine what it would be like to deliver a baby in the same area in which I had just freaked out about sinking into trash up to my thighs.

My new friend would have her baby here, with no running water, no immediate access to medical help, no sanitation efforts . . . just a trash dump. When we finished our conversation, we gave her some money so she could deliver her baby in the local hospital. As we walked away, I was appalled that this was normal for hundreds and probably thousands of babies around the world, born into families eking out a daily existence in trash dumps.

While I was touched by this woman and her living conditions, I didn't see any means by which Saving Moses could readily improve the birthing and living arrangements for moms, babies and toddlers at that trash dump. And even though it was obvious that the environment wasn't ideal for babies and toddlers, I also concluded that the most urgent survival needs were being met, albeit at very low standards.

I continued to sand away at the block of marble, exploring, learning and looking around the world for urgent needs associated with babies and toddlers. During my exploration season, there was a significant earthquake in Haiti, in January of 2010. That earthquake was devastating to a country that was already living in squalor and poverty. And I was keen to see what the needs would be for babies and toddlers on the heels of that catastrophic event. Maybe I could continue to sand away and identify who was in the marble block by joining some relief efforts in Haiti.

After some research, I came to understand that there were no nationalized immunization programs for Haiti, at that time. Consequently, many of the babies were contracting diseases that had largely been eradicated in developed countries. After learning of this, we were able to make some headway by connecting with International Child Care (ICC) to assist with extensive immunization work.

I was very pleased with the Haiti project in light of the earthquake that had just split the island, and we were able to send more than $20,000 to Haiti and make a sizeable impact by immunizing infants, the most vulnerable and needy portion of the population. I was excited to be able to help, and I started to make plans to visit Port-au-Prince to follow up on those finances and see how they were being used.

It's not an easy feat to visit a developing nation that has just been traumatized by an earthquake. And my visit to Haiti helped me to appreciate things I often take for granted: clean water, working electricity, smooth runways, functional roads and a host of other basic things that don't capture our attention in daily living. Once we overcame several hurdles, we visited a makeshift hospital clinic that was immunizing babies and toddlers. We also visited one of the tent cities that had sprung up as a result of the earthquake. There was a mobile immunization team visiting the tent city to ensure the proper protocols and immunizations for the babies and toddlers in their temporary but very extensive housing complex.

While I was extremely grateful that Saving Moses could temporarily assist with the vaccinations, I concluded by the end of the trip that there was no shortage of international attention, aid and medical support for Haiti. And I was very committed with Saving Moses to meeting the most urgent needs for babies and toddlers, where there was the least amount of aid and assistance available. I continued to chisel and sand away to search out and to reveal who was inside the marble block, so that Saving Moses could be its best self.

Around the same time that I visited Haiti, I also made a trip to Albania, a country that I'd always wanted to visit. This country had interested me for decades for lots of reasons:

- *It's in Europe, but off the beaten track*

- *It was the most inaccessible country in Europe during the Cold War*

- *Mother Teresa was Albanian*

- *It's one of the poorest countries in Europe*

For these reasons and more, I was interested in evaluating the possibilities for Saving Moses in relation to the urgent survival needs of babies and toddlers. From my research, I learned that Albania is mostly a Muslim country, and when a girl gets pregnant out of wedlock there are huge familial, social, economic and medical obstacles for her. Consequently, it's not uncommon for an unwed mom to deliver and then abandon her baby in the hospital to avoid the social and familial fallout that can accompany the unwed-mother challenge.

To support these abandoned babies, an organization was established and was the defining essential for the babies to survive. While I was in Albania, I had the privilege of visiting the hospital where this organization does its daily work. My absolute, hands-down favorite part of my entire visit to Albania was getting to meet almost a dozen of these babies who had been abandoned.

One of the babies, Granite, was around 4-6 months old and a crazy-cute little man! For Granite's situation, the police had called the hospital and talked with someone in the ward for abandoned babies and asked if they could bring over this newborn boy. The police explained that he had been found on a park bench and they were unable to find a mom or relative that would take responsibility for him. When the police brought Granite to the hospital, the staff assessed his physical health and determined that he was probably around 7-10 days old and had been well cared for. When they tried to feed him a bottle of formula he initially resisted, demonstrating that he had been breastfed during his brief life.

Granite was being well cared for in the hospital as the organization was working diligently to find a home for him, and process his adoption papers. Granite is a classic example of the rest of the babies in that ward, each abandoned but cared for until a more permanent arrangement could be resolved.

The future for the abandoned babies who are brought to that hospital is pretty good considering the rocky beginning of their young lives. Consider that for many of those babies, their moms may have quietly left them at the hospital at night, or their moms came to the hospital to deliver their baby and then decided they couldn't face such a scary and uncertain future, devoid of family or social support. And some babies are like Granite, who was brought to the hospital by the police.

In that valuable season of sculpting Saving Moses, we were able to provide resources to ensure that staffing was available to place those babies in loving homes, or to find adoptive families who would raise each baby as their own child. The staffing component for that process was a vital necessity to provide the best placement and care for those babies, and Saving Moses was very privileged to play a small part in the life of each one, for a short but significant time.

Albania provided a powerful opportunity for me to see what it could look like for an abandoned baby to receive loving care and nurturing attention, while waiting to be more permanently settled into a loving home and family. For a season, Saving Moses financially supported the key staff members who were responsible to find and place each baby in a loving family. I'm very pleased that we were able to meet that need. It was a critical part of our journey - some of the sanding, sculpting and shaping process that was an integral part of defining Saving Moses.

My next trip in that same year was the ultimate experience that helped crystalize in my heart and soul who Saving Moses is. That trip changed me, like no other trip had done in my entire life.

LESSONS LEARNED

EXPLORE WITHOUT BELITTLING

Until we explore and discover, we don't know what we don't know. Let's be careful not to shame or belittle what we don't know. Those mindsets tend to restrict our willingness to explore, grow and learn.

ENJOY THE ADVENTURE!

When we are in the learning process, it can sometimes be uncomfortable, inconvenient, surprising, disappointing and perplexing. I would suggest that the journey can be as enjoyable as reaching the destination if a person doesn't get too distracted or impatient. Staying adventurous helps us find joy and unexpected pleasant surprises along the journey!

CHAPTER 3 – FROM DELIGHT TO DIFFICULTY

I find it interesting that in the first full year of the existence of Saving Moses, each trip would become increasingly more powerful for me. This happened for a variety of reasons. My team and I mapped out the schedule for the year based on the research we had done. We considered where Saving Moses could make the most impact by looking at infant mortality rates around the world.

From our research, I learned that the nations with the highest infant mortality rates are predominately in Africa. As a matter of fact, there are only two nations in the top thirty nations with the highest infant mortality rates that are not in Africa. Generally speaking, Angola is frequently at the top of that list with one of the highest infant mortality rates in any given year. Afghanistan, however, has kept the very top spot for many consecutive years.

When we began to research who was doing anything noteworthy to address these high infant mortality rates, we found only a handful of organizations. As we continued our research, I happened to mention to a friend that I was thinking of going to Angola. He told me about an organization working in Angola that we should consider for a possible partnership in this malnutrition initiative. We contacted that organization to inquire about visiting Angola and observing their work. I wanted to see firsthand what they were doing every day to save babies and toddlers. As we went back and forth through the email correspondence between our organizations, I decided to do some further research to try to understand more about Angola and why it was in such bad shape with infant mortality.

Here are some things that I discovered about Angola:

- Angola is a rather sizable country on the west coast of Africa

- Approximately thirteen million people live there

- Angola is one of the wealthiest nations in Africa due to its natural resources of oil, minerals and precious stones

- It was a Portuguese colony for approximately three hundred years

- When the Portuguese left, there was a leadership gap

- The Cold War had a tremendously negative impact on Angola

- Angola underwent thirty years of civil war, ultimately with two main groups struggling to be in leadership

- Angola's civil war was extremely brutal and left millions of people dead and millions of land mines strewn throughout the nation

- The civil war left Angola severely debilitated, affecting economy, education system, communication and transportation systems, as well as social and familial impacts

This information was a good starting point to help me understand Angola in very broad strokes. When I began to look at specific reasons for its chronically high infant mortality rate, I couldn't find very much beyond "malnutrition." This word, "malnutrition," is frequently used to describe the challenges associated with infant mortality. And because it is so frequently used, it can be difficult to understand its scope and impact.

While preparing for my first visit, I speculated that Angola probably didn't have a nationalized infant immunization program. I thought that Saving Moses might be able to help along those lines, like Haiti, but I figured that I would wait until I could see Angola for myself before making any concrete decisions. My team and I began to prepare to visit and gauge the needs of this war-torn nation. I had a gut sense that Angola would be a very intense trip in terms of caring for babies and toddlers, especially compared to the countries I had visited so far with Saving Moses.

My gut sense played out to be accurate, even from the outset of trying to get an entrance visa for the country. For many nations, a visa is acquired by filling out an application and sending in a passport with a processing fee to the embassy or consulate of the country to be visited. In contrast, the process to obtain a visa for Angola is certainly the most difficult procedure I've ever endured in traveling to over fifty countries!

To get a visa for Angola, a person must go through the customary visa application process, as well as obtain an invitation letter, fingerprints, Portuguese translations, consulate appearances and more. Even after jumping through all those hoops, over half the time my visa has been denied. Even after all this time, I still find the visa process for Angola to be ridiculous and have walked away many times exhausted, frustrated and empty-handed.

After jumping through these hoops to get a visa, I finally landed in Luanda, the capital city of Angola. I had traveled that far by myself and the plan was for me to meet up with the potential partner organization and also my friends, Steve and Todd, who were responsible for taking photos and video for the trip. I landed early in the morning, collected my luggage, and was delighted to see Steve and Todd as I exited the customs area. At that time, I also met Niels, our driver for the week, and Joy, the hostess for our team, who would be hugely helpful in a myriad of ways. I didn't really know what our plans would be for the week, so I hopped in the truck and off we went, to where and what I had no idea!

We drove through lots of traffic in Luanda and I began to get to know Joy and Niels, such thoroughly delightful people. We drove and drove and drove, and then finally made our way out of the city and into the captivating countryside, which was beautiful in unique ways that I had never before seen or imagined.

When we were out of the city, Joy and Niels explained that if I needed to make a pit stop for a bush bathroom break, I should be mindful of any trees that had red paint on them. This meant that the area around that tree had not yet been cleared of landmines and that I should avoid finding a bush for cover in those areas. However, trees with white paint indicate that the area had been cleared of landmines and was safe. Note to self, red is bad and white is safe – good to know these helpful tips about this country!

As we continued to drive, I was astounded by the immensity and beauty of Angola. After we left Luanda, I rarely saw any power lines or cell phone towers, and there were virtually no paved roads except the one on which we were driving. I did see lots of trees with red or white paint, several old and burned-out tanks along the side of the road, and captivating landscapes complete with some amazing trees called baobabs.

These trees look like God pulled them up by their roots, turned them upside down and planted them in the ground, top down. They are thoroughly breathtaking, particularly against the backdrop of rolling hills. I saw spotted bushes and vegetation, juxtaposed with dirt that was either red or light tan. And I noted during our drive that there weren't many villages or much evidence of either human or animal life.

There seemed to be endless horizon with some speckled shacks or roadside, makeshift fuel provisions. I figured out that the plastic liter bottles with yellow fluid, displayed on rickety tables or haphazard racks, were actually for sale as a means of kindling for daily needs such as lighting a fire for cooking, or for heat.

We continued to drive and after about eight hours or more we finally arrived at our destination. Our drive was a thoroughly magnificent way to survey some of the landscape of this amazing country.

We settled into the guest house that we would be staying in and I tried to get a good night's sleep in anticipation of the next several days of seeing what infant mortality looks like in human form.

Upon waking, eating a quick breakfast and getting organized for the day, we visited a nearby malnutrition clinic for infants and toddlers. As I was getting ready, I wasn't thinking too much about what I would see or learn that day, probably because I was still in jet-lag mode and just trying to get the basics done for the day: brush my teeth, shower, drink coffee and put on clean clothes.

My first visit to this malnutrition clinic was hands down the most dire situation I had ever seen and I was completely unprepared for what I would find. When I got out of the truck for this first visit, I'll never forget what Niels, our driver, said when I asked why he wasn't coming in with us. He explained that he had already seen what was in those clinics and he had no interest in letting those sights settle into his mind and facilitate nightmares in his sleep. When he said that, I wondered what I had gotten myself into with my ready, shoot and aim strategy.

I braced myself and entered the first small and rustic, one-room building. It was dark inside so it took some time for my eyes to acclimate to the meager lighting from only a few windows. As my eyes adjusted, I saw that the little building was filled with about a dozen beds, which were closely squeezed together, and several moms were sitting on them next to their babies or toddlers.

The first infant I met was Antonio who was about four weeks old and had a cleft palate. His mom had traveled for a week and a half and left five kids at home, to bring her son to the malnutrition clinic and try to get some help for him. Antonio was clearly in a very bad state as he wasn't able to properly feed because of his cleft palate.

The manager of the malnutrition clinic explained to me that he didn't think there were any doctors residing in Angola who knew how to do cleft palate surgeries (In my early days of exploring and research, Angola had less than one doctor for every 1,000 people). Nevertheless, the staff members at the clinic were trying to see if they could find someone who could do the much-needed surgery to help Antonio. In the meantime, he alternated between whimpering and crying because of his hunger. I was completely overwhelmed, and this was just the first baby I would see.

Slowly, I moved to each bed and briefly met with each mom and her baby. Through my interpreter, I asked about her baby or toddler. This was my first immersion into the daily realities of malnutrition in babies and toddlers. I was seeing, smelling, hearing and feeling the effects and various degrees of malnutrition. I smelled the acrid trace of stomach bile and diarrhea, which are after-effects of a baby whose digestive system has been compromised and is not absorbing nutrition.

I think that for many of us, especially Westerners, it is very difficult to wrap our heads around what malnutrition means, its effects and how it happens. Many of us live in very blessed places and it is hard to truly understand how a person, much less a baby, could have their life cut short, or their future and potential decreased, because of a lack of food or proper nutrition.

As I talked with these precious mothers, I began to fully appreciate the magnitude of the challenges that these moms face. I also thought about my own pregnancies. In the season when I was pregnant and having my children, I birthed three babies in a little less than three years. That means that when I was pregnant with my second baby, I was still nursing my first child. The same was true with my third baby. During my third pregnancy, I was nursing my second child. For approximately two years, I was feeding three people (the baby in my tummy, the one who was nursing and myself).

I remember how my body felt – depleted and exhausted. I thought about the moms that I was meeting in Angola and wondered how many of them were also feeding three people. But their situation was significantly harder, and even life-threatening because they did not have the same access to medical care, prenatal vitamins, healthy food or calorie intake.

For these reasons, many of the babies that I met were in a very desperate state. Some had severe dehydration, others had amoebic dysentery, some had typhus or malaria, and some seemed just downright fat, which was perplexing to me. I didn't fully understand, so I asked about the seemingly overweight babies. I learned that what seemed like fat was actually water retention from a vitamin and protein deficiency. As such, those babies were in just as severe a plight as the ones who were visibly emaciated.

I was surrounded by the effects of malnourishment. I felt it when I touched their little bodies. I was inundated and it was all I could do to take all of this in and not visibly break down. Everywhere I looked in that little building, I saw suffering babies, exhausted moms, flies and open wounds. My ears were filled with the moans of babies and toddlers who were aching from hunger, disease, poor nutrition and who knows what else. As I made my way through the dark and dank room, it reeked with the smell of vomit, diarrhea and decay. I was overwhelmed and I had to get some fresh air, so I quickly ducked out a side door.

When I slipped out that door, I plopped down on a ledge that was connected to the building. I immediately noticed another dozen or so moms on the same ledge, with their babies and toddlers. I think they probably wanted the fresh air as well. I happened to sit down next to a nice-looking mom, holding a young child who was clearly not doing well.

For the rest of my life, I will never forget that child. She was wearing a bright and happy orange sweater, even though it was plenty warm and her situation was far from happy. When I began to look more closely at her, I noticed that she seemed to be semi-conscious and almost non-responsive. I couldn't see more than her face because she was all wrapped up in a blue, printed cloth.

I asked the mom what her daughter's name was and if I could hold her. She readily gave me her daughter's name, Engevenia, and passed her to me without hesitation. In fact, it was almost like she wanted someone else to hold her baby.

Engevenia was incredibly light for her size and I began to look at her hands and fingers, so small and frail. I paused for a bit, trying to take in the possibility that Engevenia, the little girl in my hands at that moment, might die.

On the whole, I'm not an overtly emotionally expressive person, yet I couldn't help but quietly drop tears. I asked Engevenia's mom if I could unwrap her a little bit to see the extent of the malnutrition and she gave me permission. And as I write this, I am still moved to tears as I recall that incredibly powerful and totally devastating experience.

I began to push back the large quantity of the blue, printed cloth, and when I gently lifted up her orange sweater, I was totally unprepared for what I saw and felt. I put my hand on her emaciated rib cage to feel her breathing, and I just fully broke down there. I have seen lots of pictures of trauma. I have visited and seen firsthand Auschwitz, the Killing Fields, and the Tuol Sleng prison camp in Cambodia; places of indescribable torture and horror.

But as I sat there and held the fragile body of such a small child, that one significant moment in time was more powerful to me than any visit to a site where outrageous atrocities had taken place. The severity and quantity of historical atrocities always seem to take a back seat, and even evaporate, when I hold a baby who is struggling to survive.

I wanted to stop and give Engevenia back to her mom, but I felt that I needed to fully honor her struggle to live by understanding the magnitude of her malnutrition. After some moments, I began to look for her legs, which were there somewhere in the blue cloth, and I finally found her knees. They seemed to be nothing more than two bumps holding together the sticks of her legs. At that point, I couldn't ask any more questions; I had nothing to say and I was altogether undone. I held Engevenia for a bit longer and then I carefully gave her back to her mom.

I honestly don't remember what else happened at the malnutrition clinic while we were there that morning. I only remember that my first taste of malnutrition, and its effects, was almost debilitating. I was nothing less than overwhelmed and bewildered.

Shortly after my time with Engevenia, our hostess, Joy, had thoughtfully and thankfully arranged for us to take a break. We drove into a beautiful canyon with a large, calm river. It was extremely helpful to take a pause and watch the river flow smoothly and quietly, winding its way through the majestic canyon.

Joy did warn us that the river most definitely had crocodiles in it, and they had been known to attack humans who might stroll along its banks. Despite being tempted to sit on the bank and soak in the sun and beauty, while processing the events, people and babies from my morning, I opted to sit in the back of our truck. Joy had prepared a nice picnic for us, and that would be the normal lunch plan for every day of our trip.

Those lunches were always bittersweet. I was thankful to have something to eat, but equally aware that the babies and toddlers we visited every day were dying at an alarming rate for the single reason that they didn't have enough food, or the right kind of food. On many of the days, I didn't have much of an appetite and couldn't eat anything at all.

Almost every day we were in Angola, we returned to the malnutrition clinic where Engevenia was, and I would ask how she was doing. I never really connected with her mom, in part because of the language barrier (I don't speak Portuguese), but also because she seemed very detached and removed from what was happening with her daughter. I didn't understand Engevenia's mom, or her behavior, until I made another visit to Angola, which I will explain in another chapter.

LESSON LEARNED

BE PRESENT

We often try to avoid that which is unpleasant. When we don't like a situation or circumstance, we choose various methods of escape. These may include getting busy with a project, retreating into our phones, distracting ourselves with various responsibilities, surfing social media, pursuing fitness goals, getting lost in entertainment or imaginary daydreams, and a host of other escape mechanisms.

Despite what I perceive to be unpleasant, I've found it extremely valuable to be present and to engage as much as possible. Without a doubt, escape is the path of immaturity and ineffectiveness, and presence is the path to maturity and impact.

CHAPTER 4 – BULL'S-EYE!

We Get to Make a Difference!

"Why are you here?!" Gieselle was a volunteer Portuguese doctor who was using her vacation time to provide medical assistance at the rural hospital that housed the malnutrition clinic we visited. Her greeting to us was curt and abrupt. We hadn't brought any medicines or supplies to this rural hospital, and our visit seemed to be a waste of her time and attention. To put this in perspective, I later learned that six babies had died under her care within the previous 24 hours, so her greeting to us was an expression of defeat, discouragement, frustration, despondency and loss.

Upon landing at this malnutrition clinic, I felt somewhat more confident, since I had already experienced the magnitude of malnutrition, or so I thought. After holding Engevenia and touring my first malnutrition clinic, I felt confident that I could probably handle whatever else could possibly happen on this trip. Remarkably, in the recent few months, I had participated in infant immunizations for the earthquake victims in Haiti, inspected a hospital ward for abandoned babies in Albania, met pregnant moms who would deliver their babies in supremely awful conditions, along with many other harrowing events, including my introduction to the effects of malnutrition the previous day. But I was unprepared for what unfolded over the next 24 hours, when we visited a different malnutrition clinic in Angola.

After a short tour of the hospital, we focused on the pediatric intensive care room, since that would be the place where Saving Moses could be the most useful. As I walked around the room and met the moms and their babies, I noticed several empty beds. That was where I learned about the six babies who had died the preceding day. I was completely stunned as I stood in that room, knowing that six babies, six destinies, had died in less than 24 hours.

When I asked about the causes of those deaths, I learned that those babies had died, fundamentally, because they did not have the proper food. Although the explicit cause was malaria, amoebic dysentery or something else, a nutritious diet would have enabled their bodies to more effectively resist these maladies. Ultimately, if those babies had consistently been given the proper nutrition, their immune systems could have fought off those attacks. As I absorbed the gravity of what had happened in that room just 24 hours prior to our visit, I began to look around at the survivors. Some looked to be doing pretty well, as if they would probably live.

In the back corner of the room, however, I came to a bed with a little girl who was about two years old. I was told that this baby was in such bad condition that she would probably die before the day ended unless she received a blood transfusion. Her breathing was very shallow and rapid, and her tiny and frail body was emaciated. Her grandmother was there, watching over her while her mom and dad scoured the community for blood donations to save their baby girl.

Angelina was her name and as I looked deep into her eyes, I saw both life and terror looking back at me. I don't think she understood what was going on, but her pain and fear were obvious and almost tangible. When I look at her picture today, what grips me now as it did then, is the look in her eyes. Although her entire body was emaciated, in that moment her eyes were forever etched in my soul. Initially, I thought she was afraid of me because I was a stranger and because of my white skin. But the longer I stayed, the more I could see that the look in her eyes was a look of helpless desperation, her life slowly slipping away with the passing of each minute.

In an offhanded way, the Portuguese doctor asked if any of our team had an O-blood type to donate to Angelina. We quickly found that Steve, our photographer, was a match. Steve readily agreed to donate his blood, along with many of our team, since the hospital's blood bank was entirely empty.

Here are some of Steve's thoughts from when he learned that his blood type was a match and he could donate to Angelina, the toddler on death's doorstep:

"I startle out of my daze to dancing and hugging, and nurses flooding in; I was a match to Angelina? I would have never in a million years thought it would be so, but yet it was. Next the obvious question then came, 'Are you willing to give her your blood?' I felt the word 'yes' come from my lips far faster than it came into my mind, and off ran a nurse to the local market to buy an IV bag. She returned with the supplies, I am prepped and poked, and blood starts pumping into the small plastic bag lying beside me. As I sit here, the gravity of what I'm doing and what's going on catches up and, like a tidal wave, it engulfs me."

What totally rocked me was that when we arrived at the clinic that morning, our visit seemed to be a total nuisance, a distraction to the activities for the very important mission in that hospital; to save lives. Then, Steve could donate blood and hopefully save Angelina's life! Maybe our visit had both a divine timing and purpose. I remember thinking, "Today, we aren't saving Moses. Today, we are saving Angelina!" What a phenomenal exhilaration to be there when the life of a toddler was hanging by a thread and being a part of her possible rescue!

Shortly after they had drawn Steve's blood, they connected Angelina to a monitored intravenous drip to give her a fighting chance to survive. We were all thoroughly elated, and I was giddy! We watched with eager enthusiasm as Steve's life-giving blood slowly started to move into Angelina's body. Time immediately seemed to change, moving in slow motion as we waited for Steve's blood to bring life to Angelina. Of course, I wanted to see an instant transformation in Angelina. I wanted to see the terror in her eyes wane and disappear into a peaceful contentment. And, I wanted to see her relax and smile. I watched and waited.

Finally, the doctor asked us to step out of the room and give it some time for the blood to move into her frail body and begin to strengthen her organs. We happily complied and walked around the hospital compound. We met more volunteer doctors and nurses from Portugal. And while we walked around, everyone was quietly asking questions about Angelina's progress.

- Was she getting better?

- Was the blood transfusion working?

- Were there any complications?

- How soon would we be able to see an improvement?

- What's taking so long?

After some time, we returned to check on Angelina's progress, and she still didn't look good. In fact, her eyes were glazed over. When I asked the doctor about Angelina's status, she explained that some complications had developed, and she was beginning to have some mini seizures. Angelina's heart rate was still very high, and the doctor was concerned that she wasn't improving. After a few more minutes, I could tell that we were in the way of the medical staff who were trying to help Angelina. Additionally, we had a two-hour drive to get back to our guesthouse, so we exchanged contact details and promised to follow up on Angelina's progress the next day. During our quiet drive home, I prayed that Angelina would survive.

We learned the next morning that, unfortunately, Angelina did not survive. When I received the text message, I sat down on my bed and tried to absorb and process such a painful loss. As I write her story for you now, years later, I'm wiping away tears because of her unnecessary death. When I think of Angelina, I know that what really gets to me is not only the loss of her life, the suffering of her parents, the hardship on the doctors and nurses who tried to help her, Steve giving blood to save her, etc. but what really unsettles me is that Angelina is not uncommon.

Every day there are hundreds, if not thousands, of babies and toddlers who silently die from causes that are easy to remedy. Malnutrition in babies is not impossible to cure! As such, I certainly want the death of Angelina to be the exception and not the norm – and that's one of the reasons I'm so passionate about the work of Saving Moses.

I still had to tell my team the difficult news. I wanted to tell them that even though she was struggling when we were leaving, she had gotten stronger and miraculously pulled through! But on that morning in Angola, that wasn't my message. I was concerned about how everyone would take the news, especially Steve, since he had given his blood to save Angelina's life.

I didn't know how to communicate Angelina's death with any delicacy or gentleness. I felt raw, off balance, befuddled, hazy, feeble and unsettled. Ultimately, neither my friends nor I came to Africa to see babies die, and yet that is exactly what was staring us in the eyes – infant mortality, which is a grim, sobering and atrocious reality.

I pulled myself together and walked out to tell everyone that Angelina didn't make it. She actually died a few hours after we had left. In response, everyone was very quiet. Steve took some deep breaths and excused himself from the group. The rest of us just sat around the table with our own feelings and thoughts rumbling inside our hearts and minds. Todd, our video guy, went to check on Steve after a little while. I was shell-shocked; I felt like I had gone from the pinnacle of hope and excitement to the abyss of mourning and melancholy.

After some time, Steve and Todd came back and told me that they had a crazy idea. They wanted to go back to the hospital where Angelina had died to try and find her parents, interview them and find out more about Angelina's life, in an effort to make more sense of her tragic death. It was very special to me that Steve and Todd could take such devastating news and look for ways to facilitate redemption and give meaning and purpose to Angelina's death.

The longer I thought about their idea, the more it made sense, especially if we could find Angelina's mom and dad. I floated the idea by our hosts. They thought it was a good plan, so we immediately began to make the arrangements to return to the hospital.

In the meantime, I was carefully planning our return visit to ensure that I didn't show up empty-handed again. Truthfully, the only thing I had with me was the travel money for Steve, Todd and me. I figured the hospital could use the money to buy a good quantity of medicine to help at the pediatric intensive care room, and to ensure there was a good supply of therapeutic milk.

I think we all, in our individual ways, wanted to make Angelina's short life and needless death somehow more meaningful. Even so, I wasn't sure what emotions I would face upon our second visit. I was also unsure of how we would be received by the doctors and other staff there.

We arrived at the hospital and I walked through a hallway that has since become a serene corridor of reverie for me - it is very quiet and simple. Yet, every time I am in this hallway, I hear at the other end the bustle of hospital sounds: crying babies, nurses speaking Portuguese, moms asking questions and normal hospital traffic. For me, this hallway has become a symbolic transition between very incongruous worlds: the bustle of life contrasted with the stillness of Severe Acute Malnutrition. There is a surreal and spiritual connection between these realities.

I paused in the hallway for a little bit, to collect my thoughts and brace myself for the light at the end of the dim hallway. As I paused, I was quietly listening for the cries of babies, which are the cries of life in the malnutrition world. A baby that cries has enough energy to protest and make known her discomfort. But, in the world of malnutrition, a quiet baby is usually too far down the path of deterioration for an audible cry. Indeed, I never heard a sound from Angelina. I paused, instinctively, desperate to hear the cry of life. But it was quiet.

After my pause, I popped into the infant malnutrition area and was met with possible good news. There were very few babies in the ward that day and the ones who were there looked to be in pretty good shape. When I asked about the low number of babies, they explained that many of the babies I had seen earlier had improved to the point of being moved out of the intensive care area to a more transitional place, as they continued to get stronger and stronger.

The silence I had heard in the hallway was a safe silence, babies who were getting stronger with each day and not babies who were too weak to cry. Truthfully, it was a welcome relief for me to learn such good news, particularly after the tremendous emotional struggle with the loss of Angelina.

Finally, I met up with the Portuguese doctor and we both smiled sincerely and gave each other a big hug. I explained that even though we had turned up empty-handed on our first visit, we had come back with as much help as we could immediately gather. Furthermore, I had determined to go home and find ways to make a difference.

I learned that this hospital was in desperate need of various medicines for immediate treatment, and I informed my doctor friend and the nuns who lived there permanently, that we had brought them some money for this need. They gratefully received our money, and over the course of the conversation I explained that I would work on a long-term plan to provide a steady supply of therapeutic milk.

I carefully passed along to Sister Teresa $4,000 from Saving Moses to buy medicine to continue to help the infants and toddlers under the hospital's care. Sister Teresa is one of the nuns who has been a permanent fixture in that rural hospital, providing physical and spiritual support in that community for many decades. She kind of reminds me of the more famous Sister Teresa who founded the Sisters of Charity from her work in Kolkata, India.

While the amount of money may have seemed small compared to the need, I knew it would be helpful. Sister Teresa was extremely happy to receive the money and she immediately began to make a mental list of the medicines that she would purchase. That part of the visit was deeply fulfilling and rewarding and taught me the importance of being prepared to be generous when we see needs related to our mission.

After our time with Sister Teresa, we tried to hunt down Angelina's parents based on the address from her medical chart. We were told that the neighborhood Angelina's parents lived in was super close. We hoped to find Angelina's home, her family and possibly her grave.

Angelina's neighborhood turned out to be a vast field of grass that was speckled with innumerable dwellings with thatched roofs. We followed a winding dirt path and came to a mud hut where our translator began to enquire about Angelina's parents and home. We meandered along the dirt path, which was strewn with huts made of mud and grass, and friendly Angolans who were wondering about the white people tramping through their neighborhood.

The longer we looked, the more it became obvious that we would never find Angelina's parents, her home or her grave, regardless of how hard we looked. Although everyone was polite and friendly, no one knew who Angelina was or where she lived. After many fruitless enquiries, we concluded that we would not find Angelina. We turned around to walk back to our vehicles and I looked at the grand vista all around me and saw hundreds of meandering dirt trails, thousands of mud huts and a few vehicles that stood out for their contrast.

It struck me that Angelina embodied infant mortality in Angola – one of the thousands of needless deaths of infants that would slip away, but not from my recollection, and not in obscurity.

Angelina had made a profound impact on me even though I never held her, never heard about her life, never met her parents, never learned about her family and was never able to visit her grave. I only met her for a few brief but very intense hours at the end of her life, as she struggled to stay alive. Steve, our photographer, gave his blood to help her live.

And to this day I still remember her, not with fond or gentle reflection, but with the savage and brutal imprint that experiencing infant mortality firsthand has made in my heart. I don't think that imprint has as much to do with being a mom and having my own children, but rather, it has everything to do with being human.

The bull's-eye of this chapter is the experience I had with Angelina. Up to this point in my journey, I'd never encountered firsthand, the urgent and deeply compelling survival needs of babies and toddlers. This overwhelmingly intense encounter with Angelina helped to solidify in my heart why Saving Moses focuses on the most urgent survival needs of babies and toddlers, where the care is least available.

LESSON LEARNED

STAY THE COURSE

There are lots of unexpected twists and turns, and pinnacles and pitfalls that I came through on this journey. And through the experiences I describe in this chapter, I grew and learned to stay the course and take whatever step might seem to be the next step. While I knew that I was moving in the right direction with these turns of events, I didn't take any exit ramps, even though I was an emotional wreck and somewhat traumatized along the way. I've learned to stay the course.

CHAPTER 5 - UNRAVELED

"I don't think I will ever forget that little boy. I was initially struck by how small and fragile he seemed in his tiny body. You could count every rib. I was asked to go and interview his mom and talk with her about her son's condition. During the course of our conversation, as she was gently holding her little boy in her arms, she was in the midst of answering a question when she anxiously said that her son had stopped breathing and she thought he might be dead. We immediately went and got the clinic Director and he took charge of the situation. The little boy was taken into the clinic and given an IV. Yes, that tiny boy was fragile, but he was also a fighter. I don't know if he recovered."

This is what my friend, Jody, said when I asked her about her first visit to Angola and which baby had the greatest impact on her. Even as I read this now, I can't help but feel the weight and uncertainty of every baby who is fighting to survive another day. Jody was changed by her experiences in Angola.

As such, some experiences in our lives totally change us, and what happened to me in Angola in 2010, was exactly that: life-changing! When I returned home, I had the normal jet-lag challenges, but recovering from my first visit to Angola had nothing to do with jet lag. In fact, the easy part of coming back to my life in Denver was my body switching back to the Mountain Time Zone. Here is what I said in my blog, less than two days after I had been home:

"I've been home for about 36 hours and I am trying to work through some thoughts and feelings, which are rather jumbled around. It is complete bliss to get to be with my family – they are nothing less than spectacular and I am thoroughly grateful for them! At the same time, I am also trying to process the past week. When I see a baby now, I have an instinctual reaction to ask how old he or she is and how much they weigh. When the mom tells me the answers, it feels as if my heart shatters into a million little pieces and my thoughts turn to the babies I've just seen, held, touched and am trying to help survive."

Clearly, it was difficult for me to process the events and feelings from this trip. While I was in Angola, I was able to have some practical and extremely helpful conversations about the annual costs associated with providing the life-giving therapeutic milk for the various malnutrition clinics there. I came to understand that the annual expenses for those six clinics in Angola totaled approximately $100,000. Furthermore, UNICEF had recently withdrawn their support for those clinics. When I learned about this gap, I immediately and impulsively committed Saving Moses to provide the funds needed for therapeutic milk in the upcoming year.

Immediately after I made that commitment, I silently berated myself. "How do you expect to raise a hundred thousand dollars for this? What are you thinking? You've completely lost your mind! What are you going to tell your husband? This is impossible!" I sometimes lead with my heart while my head tries to keep up. At other times, I lead with my head and ignore my heart. In those instances, I usually regret neglecting what my heart says. Still, I returned home and hoped that my head could figure out a way to keep my heart's commitment.

For several days after my return, I didn't tell anyone about my financial obligation. It was all I could do to get back into the home routine, and I needed some time and space to process all that had happened on my trip. I was also feeling extremely fragile. The first Sunday I went to church, I was struggling to appear normal and not an obliterated and emotional basket case, as I was still crying often and entirely unraveled.

Before the Sunday service began, a lady from our church gave me an envelope and said that its contents were for Saving Moses. I opened the envelope and to my surprise there was a check for $10,000! To say that I was thoroughly overwhelmed would be a total understatement. I immediately broke down and cried. I hugged her and tried to explain that she could have absolutely no idea how tremendously meaningful her gift was at that precise moment. It seemed like her gift was God's way of telling me that He was going to take care of my $100,000 commitment for the therapeutic milk for Angola. That one encounter was a powerful and tangible confirmation to me that God was most definitely involved, and that He was pleased with what Saving Moses was beginning to undertake.

It took me a few days to open up with my family and talk with them about my time in Angola and the feelings I was trying to reconcile from the events of my visit. In that season, I was also taking a graduate class on the side to learn biblical Hebrew. While I was in Angola, my assignment for my graduate class was to translate Psalm 8 from Hebrew into English – a wooden translation that would be more word-for-word and not the smooth wording that we often read in our English Bibles. As I began to work through the translation, I came to the first half of the second verse, which says,

"From the mouth of infants and nursing babes You have established strength..."

As I settled down and began to translate the verse, I discovered that the English word, "strength," in Hebrew is actually the word, "praise" or "noise." I started to muse on this and what it meant in light of nursing babes and what I had just experienced in Angola. In class, as we began to translate the Psalm, the professor came to this verse and said to me, "Sarah, I guess you heard a lot of crying babies on your recent visit to Angola."

At that point, it was all I could do to hold myself together because I immediately had a flashback of the silent hallway where I had quietly listened and waited to hear crying babies – to hear the voice of strength crying out for help, rather than the pervading silence of babies reserving their strength for another heartbeat and another breath. My thoughts and emotions were reeling, and I have no idea what happened in the rest of that class. I just know that I felt like someone had hit me with a 2x4, and I was utterly undone.

As my body adjusted to the Denver time zone, and I continued to process my trip, I had tremendous difficulty expressing my thoughts and feelings, or clearly communicating about my time in Angola. It was difficult because I struggled to find adequate words, and it was even more difficult because the people around me struggled to listen and empathize with the intensity of my journey. Thankfully, my friend Janice had walked a similar path and I had someone who understood. Janice is a seasoned photographer for a humanitarian organization. Here are her thoughts about the struggles that go with navigating First World living with developing world existence:

"Coming home from my first trip, there was a big deal about me going, from my friends and family. It was the first time I realized that some people don't want to talk about it. With tender vulnerability, I would really tell people what I saw and felt. They'd listen for a few minutes and then their faces would go blank. This would make me angry, but after a few trips, I realized that God would give me a few people with whom to share. My first few experiences with the developing world were almost unreal. Now when I go, it's harder than ever because I know more, and I know that

this is the way most of the world lives. I know that I live in a bubble, and I'm very clear that my daily life in America is a bubble. This is clear to me after doing humanitarian photography for 23 years. Various smells or sounds will trigger the memories and remind me that we are the 1% of the world. It's almost like those are my people and I don't know where I belong. I sometimes question if God wants me to move there, but capturing the stories helps thousands more. As for my family, at the beginning my parents worried about me a lot, but they're lots better now. My mom is very much a part of what we're doing. After my first trip, they were super happy that I came home safely. For my subsequent travel, I sometimes don't tell my parents everything. But then they'll find out about it from seeing my pictures and be concerned. But I downplay some of the dicey parts to help them stay settled about my travels. My parents are super proud of me and are great encouragers. My brother totally loves what I do!"

About this time, while still acclimating to being home, I picked up a book by Timothy Keller called, *Generous Justice*. In this book, Keller articulates from a biblical perspective, God's requirement to His followers to help the oppressed, weak, vulnerable and victimized. Keller beautifully walks his reader through God's expectation that His followers will be passionate about what is on His heart and in His mind, with the words "justice" and "righteousness," which flow throughout the Bible.

These words "justice" and "righteousness" in the Bible provide a very strong expectation that God's followers will act with compassion, grace and generosity to help the less fortunate members of our society – orphans, widows, foreigners and the disenfranchised. Even though it is a rather small book, it is written with tremendous intelligence and deep thought. As such, it took me a little bit of time to work my way through such deep reading. Additionally, I needed to process the emotional confrontation that I experienced as I read.

Between the reading of that book, my Hebrew class, and my trip to Angola, I was unraveled for about two months. I was also at the point where I needed to decide if I was going to pursue my doctorate in biblical languages, as I had really enjoyed my studies in Greek and Hebrew. Clearly, I was overwhelmed with all of these pursuits, convictions and choices.

Eventually, I came to the conclusion that I needed to make some decisions about where I was going to focus my attention and effort, in order to be as effective as possible. I knew that I couldn't treat my biblical languages studies as a hobby, nor would it be right to frame Saving Moses as a side project. There wasn't enough of me to pursue both and do them well.

Although my husband was very supportive, I could see that studying for a doctorate and giving Saving Moses my passion would leave virtually nothing for my family. I knew that I needed to choose between Saving Moses and a doctorate in biblical languages, since my family has never been optional on my list of priorities.

As I considered this choice, it became very clear to me that if I were to proceed with my doctorate it would be a selfish decision in contrast to giving my passion and energy to Saving Moses. After much thought and prayer, I decided to let go of my pursuit of a doctorate in biblical languages and to direct my full energy and passion to Saving Moses.

As I worked through this decision, I also had some helpful follow-up conversations with my friends who were providing the therapeutic milk in Angola. I became a little more settled in my thinking, emotions and planning for the future, and I prayed and thought about the realistic amount of money that I felt Saving Moses could commit to the therapeutic milk project. After much consideration, I solidified my commitment for Saving Moses to provide $100,000 annually to buy therapeutic milk for the six malnutrition clinics in Angola. My friends in Angola were super gracious and appreciative of Saving Moses' commitment.

I finished up the 2010 year seeing Saving Moses grow from a bleary and hazy concept to a life-changing reality. When I look back at that particular year, I can easily see God's hand leading the progress, events and development of Saving Moses. The marble sculpture had certainly taken a more definite shape. It's nice to take a look at things after the passage of time to gain new perspective. It's also noteworthy that living through such a meaningful year of tremendous highs and lows was absolutely life-changing for me.

I am extremely grateful that I didn't start with Angola, but that God gradually walked me through the increasingly difficult moments of the year, culminating with the events in October, November and December. These events included my experiences in Albania and Haiti, ending with the strategic and life-changing events that happened to me in Angola.

As I finished up the remaining days of the year, I felt like I definitely had my work cut out for me. Raising $100,000 in 2011, increasing the visibility of our essential mission, and becoming more effective in communicating our vision, along with growing our home team would be a massive undertaking! I wanted to make Saving Moses increasingly viable and effective, which would require a lot of work and even more of God's grace and provision.

LESSON LEARNED

MAKE HARD DECISIONS

When I thought about the decision between choosing a doctorate in biblical languages or saving babies, it was a wrestling match between being selfish and being generous. Just because a decision is hard doesn't mean that we shouldn't make it.

CHAPTER 6 - GROWING PAINS

As the calendar turned from 2010 to 2011, the reality of raising $100,000 to feed those desperate babies seemed almost impossible. I found myself fluctuating between the memories of their feather-light bodies in my arms, the desperation in the eyes of their moms and the dogged determination to make a difference. When I thought of the monstrous task of raising $100,000, it seemed overwhelming on a good day and ludicrous on the not-so-good days. I tried to console myself by dividing $100,000 into twelve months (about $8,333) but that didn't seem to help very much.

When I told my husband about the commitment I had made, I could tell that he was torn between being supportive and letting his engineering mind try to figure out if and how this could be accomplished. Everyone I talked with had the same question, "How are you going to raise $100,000?" Of course, I didn't have any good answers, but I was firmly committed to doing my level best to make my commitment a reality.

By the end of January, I still hadn't figured out an effective way to raise the money, though I was still encouraged by the memory of the incredibly generous lady from church who gave me $10,000 when I first returned from Angola. In my heart, I was confident that God would help me reach that goal. In the meantime, some friends were starting to create the essential components to help us spread the word about Saving Moses. These included: developing a website, creating TV promotions, and beginning the application for 501(c)3 status with the Internal Revenue Service, along with many other important things.

I still had a pit in my gut. "How the heck am I going to come up with $100,000 over the next twelve months?" I asked myself. While I didn't have any immediate answers, I decided to take just one day at a time and be diligent with my immediate responsibilities. While it may seem easy enough to simply begin raising awareness of Saving Moses' commitment through the different media platforms and audiences to which I have access, I also value that I am a part of a broader team.

For this reason, I always want to be respectful of my mom who teaches the Bible on TV and my husband who pastors our church in Denver. I take very seriously my responsibilities to support their respective ministries, goals and dreams; balance being the operative word.

Whenever I had the chance to talk about Saving Moses, I was always keen to share my experiences in 2010, as well as our plans for 2011. Seeing firsthand the needs of babies in places like Albania, Haiti and Angola, empowered me to be a passionate voice for the lives of these babies. Just because a person isn't born in a wealthy nation doesn't mean they are less valuable. With this in mind, I also began to look into other areas of need for the 0-5 age group, subsequently learning about the enormous range of need for babies and toddlers. I still get seriously overwhelmed seeing and hearing of all the needs, such as immunizations, protection from exploitation, food, essential healthcare and loving nurture, to name a few.

I was very motivated to begin planning a strategic travel itinerary for 2011. With regard to the infant mortality rates around the world, Africa is on the front lines of this battle. The statistics show that approximately eight out of ten of the nations with the highest infant mortality rates are in Africa *[1]*. From my research, I found that those babies are dying from a lack of what we would consider to be the most elementary needs, such as food and basic medical care.

Another element that would greatly help these communities is simple maternal education. Because I like to dream big, I began to look into the possibility of visiting other nations with high infant mortality rates, to consider the ways in which we might be able to make a difference on this continent. Some of the nations I am interested in to expand our work include Somalia, Sierra Leone, Mali, Niger, South Sudan, Afghanistan, the Democratic Republic of Congo and others where the infant mortality rate is high. I have big dreams to meet big needs.

Still, my first hurdle was the $100,000 commitment I had made to Angola for 2011. I also knew that I needed to get into Asia to consider the various needs that exist there. As you can imagine, those needs are quite different from the needs in Africa. I began to think, research and pray about Asia, and soon discovered some very interesting information and opportunities. The journey for our Asian outreach with Saving Moses has been extremely interesting and that's what I write about in part two of this book!

I decided that our return visit to Angola would be in the Fall of 2011 and hoped that I would have some provision and an answer to my $100,000 commitment well before then. I didn't have to wait long. In the early months of 2011, I was waiting to pick up my kids from school and the

[1] https://www.infoplease.com/world/health-and-social-statistics/infant-mortality-rates-countries

[2] https://www.cia.gov/library/publications/the-world-factbook/rankorder/2091rank.html

phone rang. When I answered, it was a very nice lady who briefly explained that God was directing her to send $110,000 to Saving Moses. That was a completely random and out-of-the-blue phone call – totally unexpected. I was thoroughly blown away!

After I caught my breath I began to cry and explained to her how I had made the commitment to Angola but had no idea how I could keep the promise. She was very gracious and explained that God was really pleased with our work and was confirming His pleasure with that financial gift. Our conversation was fairly brief and after I hung up, I just sat in the car for a while. I cried and thanked God as I soaked in what had just happened.

To say that I was dumbfounded would be a severe understatement. I had to let the conversation sink into my brain for a while, and then I called my husband and shared with him the good news. He too was totally flabbergasted with nothing short of pure amazement. We both thanked God for being so timely and so generous!

About a month before that phone call, I had made arrangements to begin sending to our field partner in Angola, a little more than the $8,333 a month so we could fulfill our commitment for the year. When we originally implemented the plan to send the monthly gift, I hadn't the foggiest idea of how I would fund that obligation, but I figured that I needed to start sooner rather than later.

We would just take it one month at a time and see what God would do. I was trusting Him to give me some creative ideas and new opportunities.

Sometimes I think that God asks us to take a step of faith when there seems to be no ground on which our foot can land, trusting that He will put the ground under our feet at the time we need it to be there. Such was the unexpected phone call from the very kind and generous lady; to this day I am still blown away by how all of this transpired. That means of provision strengthened my faith and confidence in God's hand and pleasure with

Saving Moses and our future. I knew that I had His blessing to proceed and that He would help me.

When I began to plan the return trip to Angola, I thought it would be helpful to have a friend go with me, in addition to our photographer and videographer. By now I am a relatively savvy traveler, but trips can be even more powerful when you have someone with whom to travel. Enter Jody, my friend whom I cited in the previous chapter. I've known Jody for more than 30 years, and because we've known each other for so long, she knows that I can be impulsive and it doesn't freak her out. She's the perfect traveling companion! I asked her one time, with only a few weeks' notice, to come to India with me for a weekend and she did! You'll read about that adventure later in this book.

In the last quarter of 2011, I took Jody, along with our photographer and videographer, with me on my second visit to Angola. As we drove to our largest malnutrition clinic, I found myself getting jittery. I remembered the feelings and events from that first visit; seeing, holding and facing severely malnourished babies for the first time in my life. I was also concerned about my friend Jody and her introduction to such a totally alien and unbelievable world that is thoroughly foreign to the average American existence. I wanted to be sensitive to her thoughts and feelings because a person's first exposure to malnutrition in those clinics can be extremely difficult.

Upon our arrival, I sat in the truck for a moment to collect my feelings and take a deep breath. I thought, "Here we go, Sarah. Lean into God for strength and help." Then I got out of the truck and put one foot in front of the other. As we walked up to the first of the three small white buildings of the malnutrition clinic, we greeted the various moms who were sitting on the ledge, in the shade outside of the small building. Each mom was there with her baby who was participating in the therapeutic milk feeding program. A specific program is designed for each baby based on their weight, age and condition.

Whenever I get to meet suffering babies and their moms, I am always overwhelmed with compassion, love and affection. It is impossible for me to look into the eyes of the moms and grandmoms and not be astounded by their tenacious love, especially when I hear about the extreme obstacles they overcame to get help for their babies. I also find myself sharing a common maternal love and knowing that we would do virtually anything to help our child survive and thrive. When I get to meet these moms, I am in awe that I get to make their acquaintance, hug them and in a small way get to know them.

After some quick introductions, I took a deep breath and dove into the first small white building; the building that housed the babies who were in the worst condition. I saw in the first bed a very weak little baby who was obviously struggling. Even though I desperately wanted to stop and talk with and love on the mom, I also kept in mind that we were just doing a brief overview and would return in the afternoon to spend lots of quality time and have more one-on-one interaction with the moms and their babies.

That being the case, I walked down the little aisle and briefly met each mom and their baby with an initial introduction. I was eager to return to get to know them better – to hear of their journey in life, the joy and difficulty of being a mom and about the current struggle with their baby in the malnutrition clinic.

We stayed for about 30 minutes to get a brief overview and then zipped away for a quick lunch. As it was on my first visit, whenever we break for lunch after visiting a malnutrition clinic, there is always a mental battle about eating food when I've just been around babies who are fighting to stay alive due to a lack of food and proper nutrition.

My malnutrition work exposes a dichotomy that digs into a vital and assumed basic essential – food. My access to food becomes glaringly obvious when I hold a baby who doesn't have the same access; these babies are light, frail and shaky. They have sunken eyes and shallow but rapid breaths when they are on the doorstep of death. All of this is in a very small body, which holds mighty potential that can only be realized if he or she can conquer malnutrition. I often do not even feel hungry at lunchtime, as I consider the moms and the plight of their babies.

After a quick break, we returned to our malnutrition work and I began to feel my stomach tighten in anticipation of meeting the babies and hearing their stories. Who will we meet? What is their plight? How can I be loving? Are we being effective? All of these questions, and more, quickly ran through my mind.

As we arrived back at the clinic, there was a big commotion and our host, Clint, went to find out what had happened. He swiftly returned to let us know that the baby closest to the front door, the first baby I had seen that day, had just died. All of us took a deep breath and tried to collect ourselves; our thoughts and our emotions. I found myself thinking, "Here we go again – infant death that could have been prevented with simple, easy, solutions; so much needless pain and suffering."

We quietly walked back into the little white building where literally thousands of babies had been sheltered over more than fifteen years. That small makeshift clinic has housed moms, babies, grief, relief, support, shock, disappointment, anger and pain. And on that day, another baby had died in one of its beds.

As I entered, my eyes adjusted to the darkness while my ears absorbed the quiet crying and grieving of moms with babies whose health was also precariously balanced between survival and death. I found the mom who had just lost her baby and I delicately walked over to her and held her in my arms.

She felt numb to me – like someone had hit her with a 2x4 and her body was just stiff. I held her as we watched the nurse wrap up the tiny, emaciated body of her baby girl, who had been less than three months old.

The nurse was gentle, but confident, and it was clear to me that she had become proficient with this procedure. It was an ample blanket for such a tiny body. While the nurse wrapped up the baby girl, another worker completed the paper file with the time of death.

Time seemed to stop, and we were all suspended in that surreal moment that was empty; devoid of breath, energy and future. After the workers finished their tasks, they handed the lifeless bundle to the mom who then turned and walked out the door, emotionless, stunned and hollow. As I watched her walk away, I found myself wrestling with a range of feelings – anger, frustration, uncertainty, and despair.

We walked out of the little building and sat in the shade to catch our breath and collect our thoughts. I myself didn't really talk with anyone because I didn't have any words, just pain. For some time, we just sat there. I knew that we needed to continue with our work, and I was hopeful that we could perhaps catch up with that grieving mom after a few days.

These are Jody's thoughts about her first encounter with malnutrition in Angola:

"I would have to say that I felt quietly in shock. I had never seen so many sick children in one place and really had no idea what I was supposed to do. I just silently prayed to God and followed Sarah around the clinic as she so sweetly loved on the moms. We spent a bit of time at the clinic and then went to get some lunch. When we returned, we arrived just moments after a 3-month-old little girl had died. We were allowed to observe as the nurses prepared the body so that the mom could take her daughter back to her village. It was heartbreaking to see the pain and grief the mom was experiencing."

After some moments, we mustered our courage and turned back to the malnutrition clinic, where I noticed a really chubby baby. I quickly asked if I could hold the baby who was a beautiful, fat and healthy little girl, also three months old. What a joy to get to hold a healthy baby, especially after holding a mom whose baby had just died. That baby's name was Celestina. I handed healthy little Celestina to Jody because I felt that it would really help her to hold that gorgeous and healthy little girl after having just witnessed the death of a baby. I was able to talk with her grandmom, also named Celestina, and here is what I wrote about her on that day:

"I met a woman here in Angola today that has lived through unbelievable heartache and yet she is still full of love. Meet Celestina. Celestina has had 10 babies and all but one died before they reached their 4th birthday. The sole survivor is her daughter, Manushe, who has 2 babies – grandchildren for Celestina. Despite such tremendous heartache with her children, as well as a failed marriage, Grandmother Celestina remains beautiful in her heart and brims over with love. I asked her what advice she would give to come through hardship without heartbreak. She said that a person must be strong."

Manushe, Celestina's daughter, has two children of her own, a son named Augustino and a daughter she named after her mother, Celestina. Augustino was severely malnourished and was in the process of receiving help from the clinic when we arrived. We checked on him every day that we were in Catumbela, hoping that he would get better. After a few days, he was not improving despite the efforts of the malnutrition clinic. His situation was dire, but we dared to hope. Shortly after we returned home, we learned that Augustino did not survive. Manushe, his mom, had just become another mother in Angola whose baby didn't make it.

LESSON LEARNED

TAKE A STEP

When there is much uncertainty, it can feel like we don't know if there will be ground to support the steps we take. I have found that even though I don't always see the road when I step, there is often just enough ground and support for one step at a time.

CHAPTER 7 - WE WANT HOPE

How do you make something better when it seems to be an elusive theory juxtaposed with a merciless reality? In order to cope with my visits to malnutrition clinics, it seems like I create an imaginary dam. In my American living, I have the creature comforts and conveniences of a First World lifestyle, one in which I can hold back the unraveling realities of malnourishment and dying babies.

But when I visit countries where infant malnutrition is particularly high, my imaginary dam is obliterated with the brutal realities of stringy arms, knobby knees, glassy eyes, xylophone ribs, silent struggles and the death rattle from dying babies. I have to fight discouragement every moment when the imaginary dam is burst open.

Thankfully, there is progress, which helps me remain enthusiastic and energetic to persist! And as I think of the babies that we have saved from dying, it helps me to remember Belito, whom I met on my first trip to Angola. I want to introduce him to you because I have had the privilege of visiting him on every trip I've made to Angola, and it has been abundantly rewarding over the course of this journey.

I met Belito on that first visit to Angola, when he was about fourteen months old. He had been to the malnutrition clinic for an extended stay and was going home, having recovered from his own malnutrition. When I first saw him, he was swaddled around his mom's back, secured for her walk home from the clinic. He looked very small for fourteen months and more serious than most babies his age. His life had been hanging by a thread, and without the therapeutic milk there's a good chance that he wouldn't have made it. So, every year that I see Belito, I am reminded of the first time I met him, and of his precarious existence at that time.

Belito is very healthy and sturdy now and he lives with his dad. Whenever we first pull up to his house to say hello, he is always chilly and aloof. It takes him some time to warm up and smile. Over the course of years, Belito has only gone to school on and off because of the unstable nature of his family dynamics and the gaps in Angola's public education. I've seen him play soccer, run with his friends, smile, laugh and be a normal relaxed kid.

This warms my heart and causes the foreboding clouds of malnutrition to evaporate in the sunshine of his life and vibrant childhood. Belito helps me hold out hope that we're turning the tide and making a difference for babies like Louis, Magdalena, Ernesto, Teresa, Desorae, Antonio and thousands more.

Whenever I introduce someone to Belito, I always coach the new person about him because he can seem cold and sullen, even on a sunny day. I'm not sure why he is grumpy, but his demeanor reminds me to be loving, kind and gracious no matter what. It's a good reminder because that's who I want to be as a person; full stop. When a new person meets Belito, they sometimes have a preconceived idea that he's an energetic and grateful little guy. But Belito lives in a harsh reality, with unstable parents and caregivers, such that life isn't easy for him.

Nevertheless, I am abundantly grateful that Saving Moses could be an essential part of his early life. Just because someone doesn't have a dreamy demeanor doesn't mean that it's not worth investing in their survival or existence. I'm thankful for Belito for many reasons, one of which is the motive check he accomplishes in my soul - to love authentically.

And that's ultimately where everything gets improved and transformed - with genuine love. Over the course of these years, things have improved, particularly when I think about that first visit to Angola in 2010. At that time, I knew virtually nothing about that nation with babies dying, Severe Acute Malnutrition, and the difficulties of survival in developing world countries.

Let me give you some numbers for your consideration. In 2010, Angola competed with Afghanistan for the world's highest measurable infant mortality rate. In places such as Somalia and North Korea, it is impossible to measure infant mortality due to the limited access for healthcare workers and safe accountability. When I arrived in Angola in October 2010, that was my first, square-in-the-eye look at infant mortality.

From that point on, I made the firm determination that I would do my part to begin turning the tide against such high numbers of babies needlessly dying. From approximately 2011-2018, throughout our six malnutrition clinics, we have seen the numbers of survivors rise from around 40% to almost 85%. For the same years, we have also seen the death rate decline from about 20% to less than 10%. Some of the things that we have done to see these improvements include:

- Consistently provide therapeutic milk 24/7, 365 days a year

- Feed the moms who bring their babies to the clinics, so they don't leave before their babies are fully recovered

- Maintain a rigorous system of checks and balances for monthly accountability

I am encouraged because each number is a baby; a divine gift and destiny who is deeply loved by our heavenly Father. For instance, when I visited Ernesto in Cubal, Angola and saw his emaciated 22-month-old body, I was unsettled to my core. Ernesto had been in our malnutrition clinic for a week and was struggling immensely. His little body was weak from severe diarrhea, a really bad cough and the other effects of Severe Acute Malnutrition. His mom, Theresa, was 26 years old with three other children at home who were being looked after by her elderly mother and some neighborly friends.

Theresa wanted to leave the clinic before Ernesto's treatment was finished because she was concerned about what was happening at home, but she decided on the day I visited to stay with Ernesto at the clinic for the recovery regime. It took a lot for her to trust the nurses who know the recovery path for Ernesto, which included therapeutic milk, careful observation and some helpful medicine.

Some years, when I visit Angola, things don't look as grim as others. Some years, the rains come at the right time and with the right amount of moisture, yielding healthy crops and less compromised food supplies for moms and babies. And then there are other years that make me feel like I'm being hopelessly swept away by a malnutrition tsunami that was precipitated by a drought or ill-timed rain, which caused failed harvests of crops.

In one such year I visited three of our malnutrition clinics on separate days. At the first clinic, we arrived in the morning to find 73 babies and toddlers registered to receive care and therapeutic milk. By the end of the day, at that same clinic, there were 95 babies. On a different day, we visited another clinic about a two-hour drive from the previous clinic. When we arrived in the morning there were 98 babies and toddlers registered, and by the day's end there were at least 125 babies. One of the overseeing doctors commented to us that they hadn't seen such a swell in numbers for almost 25 years.

Seeing this firsthand is very unnerving and discouraging, and it often takes me several weeks to process my time there. With God's help, I remember that we are making headway in the battle against infant mortality in Angola, even if it is a slow and painful process to ease the babies' suffering. Thankfully, in that clinic the preceding month, only 11 out of the more than 300 babies who were there for treatment did not survive. One day, every baby who comes to one of our clinics for help will live. Until then, I am reminded to celebrate progress rather than get caught in a quagmire of discouragement.

Here are some more observations from my friend, Jody. Her insight has helped me navigate the journey:

"The encounter that has been most beneficial in terms of helping me process these trips in a constructive way came toward the end of our last trip. On one of the last days that we were in Angola, Sarah had a chance to spend some time interviewing the Director of the Catumbela malnutrition clinic. She asked him how he was able to get up and come to work each day for the past 19 years. His response surprised me. He stated confidently that about 80% of the babies that come to his clinic make a full recovery and are able to go back home. When we come and visit, we only see a one-or-two-day snapshot of the babies in the clinic. We are not there long enough to see the babies get well. It is through trying to view the clinic from the Director's perspective that I have great hope that the work of Saving Moses is making a positive difference in Angola and the lives of these babies. If I have a chance to participate in God's work through Saving Moses, then I also trust that He will help me process it."

Currently, we are looking into ways that we can more aggressively combat malnutrition for babies and toddlers in rural Angola. One of the initiatives we are considering is a remote screening plan. Instead of waiting for babies to come to our clinics when they are in desperate conditions with Severe Acute Malnutrition, some literally on death's door, we intend to go into very remote communities where the moms would have to travel the farthest to bring their babies for help.

Our healthcare screeners will assess the babies and toddlers in those remote areas for and distribute at-home rations for those babies, hopefully before they reach the stage of Severe Acute Malnutrition. With this initiative, we hope to catch malnutrition in the moderate phase to prevent it from becoming life threatening.

Democratic Republic of Congo: We have recently expanded our malnutrition work in Africa to take on a malnutrition clinic on the east side of the DRC. This initiative is particularly important because of the long-term instability in this region, which has a major impact on infant mortality in this country! This challenge has been further compounded by an Ebola outbreak in this area, creating more chaos in an already fragile and highly unstable area. All of these factors combine to make infant mortality a critical issue for this region.

Afghanistan: As I continued to research the countries in the world with the highest infant mortality rates, I was continually distressed to see that Afghanistan consistently maintained the highest position on the list. I could easily understand why it was so difficult for babies to survive in Afghanistan, in both rural and urban areas.

The political and military instability that dominates that country has existed for decades, creating havoc and mayhem that affect the population of babies and toddlers more than any other single segment of the population. Moreover, as you read this, more than 40% of the babies born in rural Afghanistan will not survive.

This is precisely why Saving Moses is active in rural Afghanistan, seeking to bring life and transformation to babies and toddlers where the need is most urgent and the care is least available. So, what do we do in rural Afghanistan and how can we be change agents in such remote places?

For starters, we do grassroots community training on healthy delivery practices and midwifery. For example, Hamad has been a father, but he has no children now because of a simple lack of education. In developed countries, we understand that a baby who is born not breathing can be given a firm slap on the backside to cause him to gasp and clear mucus out of his airway, and thereby start to breathe.

In rural Afghanistan, Hamad's children were born not breathing, but he didn't know about this procedure and had lost three babies before learning of this simple technique. Hamad is certainly grateful to know this valuable piece of information, but he's also sad for the needless loss of his three babies. Saving Moses provides such education, along with other training and midwife access to make a difference in rural Afghanistan.

Additionally, Saving Moses is providing infant vaccinations for remote health clinics, giving essential immunizations and making basic medical care accessible for moms who have no access to it, or means of transportation. No doubt it's impossible for these moms to bring their babies to larger urban areas to get more sophisticated care.

But it's dangerous for our healthcare workers to go into the rural communities as well. They face not only the opposition that can come from traditions rooted in a lack of health education and culture, but also some religious and political resistance that can even be life-threatening for them. Because of challenges such as these, we are sometimes forced to temporarily scale back our operations to keep our workers safe. At other times, we are able to take advantage of various changes to make greater headway in caring for babies and toddlers in Afghanistan. Afghanistan is definitely a challenge!

As we come to the end of this chapter, I am reminded that Saving Moses has also done several special projects over the course of its years, in various countries with urgent crises. Those projects include supporting babies who were orphaned or severely impoverished from the Ebola epidemic in Sierra Leone and Liberia, food and nutritional support for babies and toddlers under two years old in Syria and assisting with medical essentials in developing countries like Bangladesh, Ethiopia and India. And we won't stop!

At this time, we are actively working on plans to go into extremely challenging countries like Somalia, Mali, South Sudan and others. Going into places where babies and toddlers are least likely to survive and thrive is exactly where we aim to sink down our roots, in order to give them a fighting chance at life. We save babies daily where the need is most urgent and the care is least available.

LESSON LEARNED

STAY ENCOURAGED

When I look at the immensity of the need, as well as the babies who have died, it's very easy to get discouraged. If I let myself begin to reside in a place of discouragement, it's easy for me to get despondent and even become hopeless. While I acknowledge the need and memorialize the babies who have died, I encourage myself by looking at the difference we are making and remembering the babies who have survived.

♥ ✚ 🍼

PART 2: NIGHTCARE

CHAPTER 8 - WHOSE BABIES ARE THESE?

"Don't get burned on the exhaust pipes!" I thought to myself on a rainy and sweltering summer night in Phnom Penh, Cambodia. I meandered through a maze of haphazardly parked motorcycles, probably driven by drunken riders. Gas fumes permeated the humid air from the motorcycles as I made my way to the sidewalk, blinking away the rain so I could see better.

Despite the distant streetlight, everything was blurry from the rain and dense humidity. The sidewalk was pocketed with shadows and peppered with dressed-up women and drunken men leaning in for "conversation." This road along the Mekong River has loads of people, mostly tourists looking for companionship through the night. The darkness I felt was caused more by the shady environs than the sun going down for the day.

"What the heck?!" I screamed in shock and alarm, *"I almost stepped on them!"* I did a stutter step to miss the little bodies as I literally stumbled upon three babies who were sleeping unattended on blankets on the sidewalk, in the drizzling rain. Babies lying on the sidewalk at night was the last thing I expected to find as I strolled with my friends to get an ice cream after dinner. I wondered out loud, *"What are these babies doing lying out here in the rain with no one watching them?"* There were three little treasures, sleeping despite the traffic whizzing by on the road, motorcycles revving next to them and pedestrians sauntering along the riverside.

I abruptly stopped to look around for a mom or guardian of some sort, since I didn't see anyone immediately present to protect those babies. After a few minutes a lady showed up. She had glassy eyes and a dull grin and was mumbling something in the Khmer language. Maybe she was their mom. Who knows? The point remains that those babies were lying on the sidewalk unattended and exposed to all kinds of hazards and atrocities. I was appalled, stunned and dismayed all at once. How could anyone leave precious babies in such a vulnerable position?

I share this true story with you as an example of what life is like on a daily basis for the babies and toddlers of sex workers in the developing world. And from my years of providing NightCare for these babies, I now know that the sidewalk may have been much safer than the other precarious options. It's likely that their mom was earning a living as a sex worker, serving Western tourists in that seedy but prosperous neighborhood.

I first became aware of the plight of thousands of babies and toddlers as I watched the documentary, *Born Into Brothels*, filmed in Sonagachi. Sonagachi is a brothel in Kolkata, India with 20,000 sex workers in one square mile. I found it hard to wrap my brain around those numbers. It would be like 100 sex workers living (working) in one average-size U.S. home, and that home butted up to 199 more of the exact same homes; each with 100 sex workers, with their babies, toddlers and clients all crammed into the smallest of spaces.

Can you even imagine the chaos, filth, or the danger in such a situation? One scene in the documentary shows a half-naked toddler chained to a rail in a bedroom. This brief scene has run through my memory countless times and it has been one of the primary motivations for me to start NightCare with Saving Moses. Having this scene indelibly imprinted on my soul caused me to think about the lives of the babies and toddlers of those sex workers.

Who looks after the babies and toddlers? Are they in the room with their mom as she works? Are they under the bed, in a corner, or on the bed with her? Is there a place for them to go and be safe while their mom works –like in America with daycare? I began to consider these questions and imagine the night-to-night existence of the babies and toddlers whose moms earn a living in this profession, which overflows with risk, health emergencies, dangerous individuals, unsafe living conditions, sexually transmitted diseases and sanitation hazards.

The world in which we live has many atrocities, but what consistently makes your palms sweat and quickens your heart rate? What do you see or hear about around you that continually gets you upset or moves you with compassion? Usually, the things that repeatedly bother you are a good indication that God is inviting you to be a part of something bigger than yourself. Stories of people like Jackie Robinson, Nick Vujicic, and Katie Davis Majors with *Kisses from Katie* tell us about real-life people who turned their angst and adversity into something bigger and better than themselves: tragedy transformed to triumph and treasure.

I think there is a longing in each of us to make an impact with our lives – to live for more than the daily grind or the endless consumerism that plagues the Western world. We often joke about First World problems to contrast the deplorable conditions and needs of the less fortunate in the developing world. Regardless of where we live, I believe that you and I want to make our lives count for something more than the consumer mindset with creature comforts and trivial pursuits!

This is exactly what I thought as I watched the documentary on Sonagachi, with a significant twist: Most people focus on the sex workers and look for ways to support or help the women whose existence is nothing less than a living hell every day. But I was fixated on the babies and toddlers of those sex workers. Clearly, babies are a natural result of this industry, despite the various prevention methods and abortions that occur. I applaud every effort to help the women, but I had to ask, "What is being done for their babies and toddlers?"

This was the beginning of NightCare, something God put into my heart to care for and love the least of the least - babies and toddlers of sex workers in developing countries. In America, many moms work full-time throughout the day and leave their young children in daycare facilities. My thoughts went to the idea of NightCare. Rather than providing this service in the daytime, we could do it at night when the moms work - hence the term "NightCare," the beginning of a very big dream in my heart.

What are the dreams in your heart? How do you see yourself doing something noteworthy and impactful? Sometimes it's helpful to remember that making a difference doesn't always mean that you're the person at the forefront. Actually, there are innumerable people who don't have the public recognition but join the journey with those who are leading the charge. The truth of the matter is that you have distinct and important gifts and talents to make a significant impact, regardless of your public visibility.

I say this because my journey has overflowed with wonderful people who have walked with me, doing stuff that is impossible for me! These individuals have been willing to see the pain and suffering of babies and toddlers in the developing world, and they've decided to be heroes in small, medium and big ways! It's important for people to recognize atrocities and hardships, without being insensitive to human suffering. But more than recognizing such suffering and evils, they need to unsettle and even unravel you, in order to make a difference. Charity fatigue and numb indifference can cause us to be content with comfort and convenience, so much that we don't do anything. And that's why you're reading this book – because you want to make a difference!

And for me, I couldn't get away from thinking about babies and toddlers sleeping every night in brothels, under the beds where their mom is working, locked in closets and in various unsafe situations. As the idea of NightCare began to develop in my heart and mind, I started looking for organizations that were helping those babies and toddlers. I found none. Zero! Zip!!

Although there are several organizations that provide a variety of helpful resources and services for sex workers, ranging from meeting immediate healthcare needs, providing educational training and opportunities, opening doors for alternative professions, counseling and lots more, there was absolutely nothing available to meet the urgent needs of babies and toddlers while their moms work.

This is where a lot of people stop dreaming because they don't find anyone doing what they imagine. Have you faced a situation in which you desperately wanted to be a part of the solution but abandoned that dream? Did you stop dreaming when you realized that no one was doing what you envisioned? Or, maybe you quit because someone poured cold water on your fervor with words like impossible, unheard of, dangerous, impractical, etc.

It's very tempting to give up on a dream when no one else can see what you envision, but each of us must let the need and passion we feel continue to fuel the dream that's in our heart! Over the years, I've had more than my share of cold water and obstacle conversations. My first impossible conversation was a significant gut check and I almost quit before even getting started.

When I became aware of the massive need for NightCare, I did what I normally do: ready, shoot and aim! That's my way of saying that I usually leap before I look. To this end, after having seen the documentary with the toddler chained to a rail, I began to make enquiries about work being done in Sonagachi, the brothel in India with 20,000 sex workers. I located a few humanitarian organizations working with these sex workers. I was familiar with one of the organizations because I had done some educational work with them several years earlier. I learned that they ran a health clinic in Sonagachi and provided medical services to the moms on a weekly basis.

I immediately concluded that NightCare would fit perfectly with the healthcare clinic, since it operated in the daytime, and NightCare could use the same facility at nighttime. Voila! So I emailed the organization with my thoughts and proposed a partnership of sorts to maximize the use of the clinic with NightCare. Their reply to my suggestion was very positive, so I enthusiastically hopped on a plane to Kolkata, India with a few friends to launch NightCare, or so I thought.

This type of international travel isn't glamorous by any stretch of the imagination. It feels like I'm being squeezed through a wormhole when I travel overseas because of the substantial time changes, zooming through the air in a metal cylinder and landing on foreign soil, everything topsy-turvy from where I started. So landing in Kolkata at 1:30a.m., after traveling more than twenty continuous hours was definitely a wormhole experience. Upon clearing immigration, we drove through the sleepy streets and finally arrived at the guesthouse where we would stay for the next several days and I fell into bed, utterly exhausted.

The next morning, I was very eager to start the day and talk about the first steps to begin NightCare. Seated across from our hosts, we finished breakfast, exchanged the normal pleasantries and I jumped into the discussion to start NightCare.

"It's not going to happen," our host said in a flat and firm tone. I was certain that I didn't hear him right, so I said, "Sorry, but I don't think I heard you correctly. Would you please say that again?"

"What you're thinking of doing in Sonagachi is too dangerous, impractical and impossible, even though we agree with you that these babies and toddlers are in desperate need of help and protection." They acknowledged my observation about the babies being tied to the bed where their mom was working. Furthermore, they added that it's not uncommon for toddlers to be drugged and put under the bed so they don't distract the flow of clients throughout the evening. The more I listened and learned, the more appalled I became, which made me all the more committed to launching NightCare!

In my thinking, "no" often means "try again from a different angle" or "brainstorm creative solutions to overcome the obstacles." On that morning, there would be none of that. Our hosts shut down every idea, possibility and strategy that we came up with, so after more than two hours of that dead-end conversation, I was thoroughly frustrated.

When we returned to our room to collect our stuff for an afternoon excursion, my friend, like me, was in bewildered shock. I privately asked her, *"So if they knew that their answer would be so definitively 'no,' why did we come all this way and endure the wormhole experience when they could've simply given us their decline in an email?"* "Good question," she replied.

Needless to say, the next few days in India felt like a giant waste of time since there would be absolutely no progress toward launching NightCare in Sonagachi with that organization. I tried to be cordial and not surly, remembering that they were hosting us, providing a place for us to stay and a ride back to the airport. And my poor friends didn't need any more cranky from me, in an already frustrating situation. I made it through those days and finally got on the plane to return home. I was very angry because I felt betrayed and misled, having wasted time, money and energy for a seemingly pointless pursuit.

When I got home, my husband asked how our trip went. My sour and curt answer made it clear to him that I wasn't interested in talking about the fiasco. This trip happened in March of 2011 and I felt like I had chased a wild pipe dream that would never happen. That's how I tried to resolve my thoughts about the Kolkata trip, but it didn't work. The image of the toddler chained to the bed in Sonagachi kept haunting me to the point that I felt like I needed to do something about it, but what?

Obstacles and closed doors are a part of the journey of turning a dream into a reality. If it were easy, everyone would do it. If there were no hurdles, roadblocks, financial shortfalls, resistance, etc. the dream in your heart would have already been done. Easy is for average and I don't think you picked up this book because you're curious about average or common.

There's a story about a donkey who was stuck in a pit and dirt kept getting thrown onto his head. Initially, he was disheartened from being in the pit and the dirt that kept landing on his head added insult to injury. But he decided to let the dirt become an advantage, shaking it off and stamping it down until it propped him up enough to step out of the pit.

Sometimes we have to change our thinking and look around for possible solutions rather than get discouraged by the impossibilities, roadblocks and deficiencies. It's better to frame this kind of stuff as a detour rather than accept with futile resignation what seems to be impossible.

I began to think about the various connections and relationships I had near India and remembered my good friends in Phnom Penh, Pastor Jesse and Soar McCaul, from New Life Fellowship Church, whom I was already scheduled to visit in July of that year. At this point, I had known Pastor Jesse and Soar for several years. We have a strong family connection and I overflow with love and respect for them. When I sat down in their living room in Cambodia to explain what was in my heart, they had the opposite reaction from the organization in Kolkata.

"That's great, Sarah! We love the idea of NightCare! What can we do to help?"

Their enthusiasm was like wind in my sails and we began to talk about various people and organizations that provide relief and aid to sex workers in Phnom Penh. Pastor Jesse and Soar eagerly gave me the names of organizations and some important contact people - such a glorious contrast to my disappointment in India! I immediately began contacting people and setting up coffee dates and appointments to share my NightCare ideas with willing listeners. I hoped to find individuals with whom NightCare would resonate, so we could make some forward progress.

From that conversation, I had the honor of meeting Ruth, a woman whom I greatly admire. Ruth started an NGO (non-governmental organization, also known as a charitable non-profit in the international aid community), devoted to assisting sex workers who want to leave that industry and begin a new life for themselves. I'll never forget sitting on the curb of a playground, talking with Ruth as we watched her kids play.

I explained the beginning of Saving Moses, having met newborn babies abandoned in a field in Ethiopia. She interrupted my story and asked, "What were the names of those newborn girls?" I mindlessly replied, "Sarah and Ruth," and suddenly I was struck with the awareness that I was sitting next to Ruth in that moment. Perhaps God had aligned the steps and journeys for both of us, Sarah and Ruth, to make NightCare a concrete reality and not just a pipe dream in my mind and heart. We continued to talk, both of us attentive to the possibility that God had put together some interesting puzzle pieces that could lead to very powerful redemptive work!

After meeting Ruth, I also had an appointment with another gracious woman, Solida, who had also started an NGO to assist women who were trapped in the sex industry. I remember sharing with Solida, along with a few other visitors in the room, my heart for NightCare. Once we'd circled around for introductions, I learned that one of the visitors, Ann, had started and was running a daycare in Phnom Penh. I also learned that daycare was a pretty foreign idea in the culture of Cambodia, so NightCare was like talking about something on the moon! Nonetheless, Ann seemed interested in the idea, even though she was visiting Solida for an altogether different reason.

I learned that Ann was Irish. She was married and had been living in Cambodia for more than five years at that time. She was quite familiar with the culture and needs of the country. I asked if I could visit her daycare before I left because I wanted to see what it looked like under her leadership and influence. Truth be told, I was interested to see if she would consider doing the same concept, but at a different time of day and with a different group of babies and toddlers.

When I visited her daycare, I was extremely impressed with the quality of care, the cleanliness of the facility, the excellence of the workers and the overall organization of her center. Ann had a beautiful facility and I was more than satisfied that she was proficient with running a daycare.

Unfortunately, she was already settled into her work and didn't have the capacity to add on another challenge like NightCare.

I left Cambodia encouraged by the possibilities but a little frustrated with the uncertainties. On the positive side, at least I didn't have people telling me that NightCare was impossible, like the wet blanket in Kolkata, nor did I feel like I was being strung along out of polite respect. However, I didn't have any concrete next steps and that was a little frustrating.

While immersing myself in the immediacy of raising my kids, being a wife and being in full-time ministry, I kept thinking, "Now what?" At this point, my kids were going into the 6th, 5th and 3rd grades. Clearly, I already had an incredibly active life, full of responsibilities, so adding heavy projects to my already overflowing workload wasn't realistic. Still, I couldn't get away from the idea of NightCare, even though I had no idea what steps to take next.

Sometimes the dreams in our heart have to simmer for a little while so they can become more solidified in our thoughts. Indeed, cold water, delays and uncertainty can put to the test the depth of our passion and commitment to these dreams. Maybe the initial opposition can serve to develop our persistence muscle, since the future will likely have more obstacles and icy feedback, and mounds of rejection along the way!

After a few months had passed and my kids were settled into the school routine, I kept feeling a nudge in my heart to make some forward progress with NightCare. The honest truth, however, is that I didn't have the bandwidth to do the extensive follow-up and communication that was needed to pull together the loose strings and formulate the implementation of NightCare.

So in November, I asked a friend, Susan, if she would take on this project for a few months and manage the correspondence with everyone involved to see if we could get NightCare up and running. I also learned, shortly thereafter, that Ann had stepped away from the immediate oversight of the daycare and was interested in coming alongside me to do NightCare, even though this would be something entirely new for both of us!

Hearing of Ann's availability and interest in helping me with NightCare was thrilling to my heart. Could this dream really be coming together? Could there be a way to make a substantial difference in the lives of these precious little ones? Susan did a magnificent job of taking on this project, communicating with everyone and helping to get the myriad of details set up for implementation.

Be abundantly certain that the dreams in your heart will never be accomplished in isolation, or with your finite resources and talents. Actually, one of the things I've most enjoyed as I've walked this journey with Saving Moses is watching people come alongside me whose natural abilities are nothing like mine.

As you read through this section of the book, you're going to meet many outstanding people, like Susan, who have added their talents and energies in order to grow Saving Moses and make it increasingly effective. I am grateful every day for the individuals, teams, partnerships, supporters and organizations that have propelled us to ever-increasing next levels.

As you press forward to turn your dreams into a reality, be open for God to bring the necessary help you need to make it happen. Consider as well that God is likely asking you to come alongside someone else's dream. You are uniquely gifted and can add massive transformational value to make other people's dreams come true!

A few months later, I flew to Phnom Penh and hired Ann to be our National Director of NightCare in Cambodia, after sharing with her my vision to open multiple NightCare centers throughout Phnom Penh and other parts of the country. During that trip, we looked at rental properties and signed a lease on a perfect house near a slum where many sex workers lived. It's important that our NightCare centers are easily accessible to the moms.

Within three weeks, Ann had hired staff, scrubbed the house from top to bottom and had everything ready to begin NightCare. In addition to hiring the staff to provide nightly care, Saving Moses bought all of the necessary appliances (washer, dryer, rice cooker, stove, etc.), along with cribs, mats, bedding, toys and washing supplies to properly care for the babies that we looked forward to receiving each night!

Furthermore, my friend Ruth had agreed to help introduce us to the sex workers in the nearby slum so we could begin to build trust and introduce those moms to NightCare: a place where their babies and toddlers would be protected, nurtured and loved, while they worked. I was more than a little giddy!!

And so began NightCare, or at least that's what I thought on the flight home from that trip. When I think about it now, the circuitous journey to get NightCare launched was one of risk and uncertainty. Challenges of this magnitude can massacre dreams and turn them into elusive fantasies. Nevertheless, the dreams that are in your heart will inherently be dressed in the garb of risk and uncertainty. But with eyes of faith, we can look past the camouflage and see the certainty of God's plans to express genuine love through us and give eternal meaning to our temporary living.

LESSON LEARNED

PERSISTENCE

The idea of NightCare is very unique. When I first tell people about NightCare, it's not uncommon for me to get quizzical looks, skeptical questions, sometimes hostile feedback and even outrage that I would "facilitate prostitution." I recognize that we all bring assumptions, cultural biases, and both ethical and religious filters to the way we process information and how we interact with the world around us. However, it's difficult to change the world around us when we refuse to change how we see things. Conventional thinking produces conventional results. Seeing things from a different perspective allows us to think in unique ways that can often be helpful and even transformational. It's okay to see things a little differently and with a less-than-traditional mindset!

CHAPTER 9 - HOPING FOR MORE

"We have four babies? That's it??" I was really discouraged with such a low turnout for the grand opening of NightCare in Cambodia. It seemed reasonable that it would take us a few weeks to ramp up, but after a month of being operational I had expected lots more than just four babies. I'd imagined moms lining up in the street every evening with their babies and toddlers, eager and happy to trust us with the care of those who were most precious to them.

How could my imagination have been so far off? Were we doing something wrong? Did we need to do some extra work to be more visible in the neighborhoods? What did we need to do to have more babies and toddlers attending NightCare? I had a plethora of questions and decided we needed to roll up our sleeves and start problem-solving to find whatever the attendance obstacles might be.

Have you ever had a dream in your heart that felt tangible to your hands and feet, but invisible to your eyes? Even though my imagination could see our NightCare center overflowing with babies, the day-to-day reality didn't match what I saw in my heart. And many times, this is where people can get discouraged, lose focus and even quit. I can appreciate what it feels like to be discouraged, but it's vital to allow our vision and passion to be persistent in turning the impossible into the probable, and ultimately, into reality. Let's be careful not to quit before we've hardly started!

Even though I was discouraged by the lack of results, I wanted to understand these moms, their thought processes and their priorities. I began interviewing the few moms who had decided to bring their babies to NightCare. One of our babies was a two-year-old girl whose mom worked not only at nighttime as a sex worker but also during some days, collecting and recycling garbage in an effort to make ends meet.

Because she was gone a lot, various people would look after her two-year-old daughter. One afternoon, a regular evening client had been pressuring this mom for extra time and she declined his advances. After lots of pressure, the client became very angry and decided to punish his girlfriend by throwing acid on her daughter, the two-year-old toddler attending our NightCare.

Shortly after the attack, I was able to sit with this mom and her daughter whose face would be scarred from the acid for the rest of her life. As I talked with her through the interpreter, I learned that not only had this client thrown acid on her daughter, but he had also sexually molested her, doing things that horrified me and left me with a holy anger. I was entirely repulsed by the depravity of this man, that he could perpetrate such evil actions against an innocent little girl. And because the mom was so poor and uneducated, she didn't have access to financial or legal resources to bring him to justice.

When I enquired about the possibilities of prosecuting the man, I was even more outraged to learn that such behaviors are not uncommon in the developing world. And the legal processes can frequently be inaccessible, corrupt, inadequate, overwhelmed and sometimes too outdated to administer justice in cases like these. Getting justice and fair access to legal assistance is a challenge, no matter what country a person lives in.

In another interview with a mom who was bringing her four-month-old daughter to NightCare, I was able to visit her home to ask questions and broaden my understanding of her situation. I immediately noticed that when I was talking with this mom, she was extremely distracted, and her answers were very quiet and short.

As I carefully watched her, trying to understand what was happening in her mind, I noticed that her eyes kept looking out the window and down on the street. I followed her gaze and saw a man looking up at her from the street with a menacing and evil look. Slowly, I began to piece together what was happening. The guy looking up at her had malicious intent. Her short answers and nervousness likely came from the fear she had from watching the threatening guy.

Furthermore, I began to understand that my friends and I were Caucasians in the midst of a Khmer slum. We didn't exactly blend into the general population. Instead, we were the proverbial zebra in a herd of horses. The longer we lingered, the more agitated the woman became. I decided that we should quickly finish our time with her, hoping to minimize any potential danger or threats she might face.

I asked a few days later if she was doing okay and learned that the man on the street was the slumlord. He was paying close attention to our visit with this mom and she was very aware of his focus on her. It was good that we didn't stay long, and I was relieved and very thankful to learn that both the mom and her baby daughter were safe, with no ill consequences from our visit.

From these interviews and more, I began my slow education in the day-to-day living of sex workers in the developing world. The conversations I had with various moms started my learning process for some of the fundamental components of how they think, their priorities and daily living.

While it seems glaringly obvious now, over time we came to appreciate that trust is a platinum currency for these moms. Earning their trust is not only difficult, but also takes lots of time and integrity. The results of this truth became painfully clear as the weeks wore on with NightCare and we continued to care for only a handful of babies. From various mothers among the sex workers in the slums, we would hear questions like:

- "Are you going to kidnap my toddler and sell her into the sex industry?"

- "Are you going to kill my baby and sell his organs on the black market?"

- "Are you going to hurt my baby when you give her a bath?"

These questions, along with others, left me heartbroken as I came to better understand the deplorable conditions and suffering these moms and their children have known in their daily existence. I also began to think about the neighborhoods where these moms live with their babies, because of my close contact with the moms I described above. I could sense that both of these moms, despite their best efforts, were frazzled by their daily living.

Often, when we begin to step into places and situations that can be overwhelming, we want to quit. Or we think that our meager efforts are meaningless in such a massive galaxy of need and depravity. Unfortunately, many people who have been inspired and motivated to do something significant quit, sometimes at the first blush of resistance or difficulty. As I said earlier, if something meaningful were easy, it's likely already been done. So here is some simple wisdom: don't quit.

I say this because the more you learn about what makes you agitated and upset, the better equipped you'll be emotionally to endure hardship and make a significant impact. You will also, because of increased information, be able to develop wise plans on how to proceed.

By asking questions and seeking to understand, I learned that the neighborhoods where my moms live are seedy and dangerous on a good day. For example, we affectionately call one of the neighborhoods "Plankville" because it is situated on planks over a river or open sewage conduit, depending on your perspective.

The sewage there rises and falls depending on the season of the year, and it sometimes overflows onto the plywood floors of the shanties in which these families live. This whole neighborhood sits on top of rickety piers, and the narrow alleyways between the corrugated tin shacks are nothing more than wood planks, sometimes nailed to the sideboards that are affixed to the vertical piers.

You know there has been an upgrade in the neighborhood when the worn and broken wood planks are removed and replaced with new and more sturdy strips of wood. These also will soon be worn down, broken and inevitably missing.

And the smell by far exceeds the stench of a laundry basket full of sweaty gym socks! What's worse is that this stench isn't just restricted to a small locale where a person could hold their breath and get away from it. The stench is pervasive, seeping into your clothes and hair, such that when I return to my hotel room, my clothes need laundering before the odor saturates the entire room - a lesson I learned from experience. This is kind of like the pervasive and long-lasting smell from skunk spray.

It's interesting that no one who lives in Plankville seems to be remotely bothered or aware of the odor. Instead of being agitated by the stench, the residents, even when it's summertime and sweltering with sticky heat and humidity, stand in the doorways of their shacks and casually fan themselves. And of course, the stench seems to amplify in the heat, as if that were possible.

In the summertime, it can almost seem unbearable because everything bleeds into a sweaty and smelly mess, dripping and oozing with the scent of rotting flesh from animal carcasses, rancid fruit and fetid refuse. To this day, often when I smell something odious, I'm instantly transported back to Plankville in my thoughts and memories with an almost visceral retching.

Despite the stench, heat and substandard conditions over the course of many years, I love getting to visit this neighborhood and I hate it at the same time. This is one of the things that happens when we settle into doing something meaningful, and we've decided not to quit. We grow to love the people despite their flaws and humanity, and we return even though the conditions can be less than appealing.

I love getting to see my moms and their babies who are growing into kids. I hate seeing a toddler pick up a candy from the dirt and pop it into his mouth, unwashed and covered in ants. I hate watching a baby slip through the cracks in the planks and drop into the sewage below, hopefully to be fished out by a nearby neighbor who might see and extend a hand to help. But when all the dust settles and I get accustomed to the sewage, stench and humidity, my Plankville is about the people, far more than the deplorable conditions.

Every year we take a team to Cambodia to see firsthand and participate in NightCare, so it's not an idealized or ethereal concept. As you read about NightCare, I also want you to know the feelings and observations of various team members who have come with me over the years. Here are Morgan's thoughts about the various neighborhoods she has visited:

"When you walk the neighborhoods, there are things that stand out, like the smell of rot and decay as you walk over the equivalent of a landfill, or the black sludge of sewage that runs underneath the homes. These things become secondary to me when I walk into a home and see how a mom pays to live on five planks of wood with two walls and a half-roof. The surface paints a picture of extreme poverty and unlivable conditions. When I look deeper at the picture though, I see a community that cares for one another because no one else will. I see generous mothers who are happy to share what they do have with a complete stranger. It makes me sad to know so many live in those circumstances and that these children are growing up at risk of numerable things because of where they live. At the same time, I have never experienced community and generosity like I have walking through these neighborhoods."

As I've watched many of the Plankville inhabitants, I've often wondered about why they seem to be indifferent to the help we've offered to their babies and toddlers. Truthfully, sometimes the dream that God puts in our heart isn't embraced with eager gratitude by the recipients and this can be very disheartening. Often times, those to whom grace and genuine love are offered can be distrustful, disrespectful, sometimes hostile and even combative.

I've seen more than a few people give up sharing love and hope because the recipients weren't appreciative or willing to receive such generosity. This can make it difficult to persist because it seems like our generosity should be eagerly welcomed! But this often isn't the case for various reasons, one of which is the environment in which folk live. These unstable and dangerous surroundings reinforce fear, distrust and the most basic transactional living.

As we work in places like Plankville, we learn a necessary ingredient for being a part of something that is bigger than ourselves: we must be deeply moved and touched at our core; disturbed and moved in ways that remain concrete in our souls and don't evaporate with the mundane, and the comforts of our daily living. Of course I'm affected by the sights, smells, humidity and dirt, but there's a noteworthy reason to return, in spite of the living conditions and poverty: the people.

I find that many Americans are entirely overwhelmed, initially, with the horrific living conditions, so much that they miss connecting with the people who live in these abysmal conditions. There is a difference between being grossed out by the awful sights and smells and being unhinged at the core, to the degree that we begin thinking of ways to make a difference and cause lasting change.

When you dream about doing something impactful and significant, I would strongly encourage you to think in terms of people more than projects, and individuals more than achievements or accolades. I say this as I'm reminded of the choice that Mother Teresa made when she received the Nobel Prize for Peace in 1979. Rather than accept the traditional banquet that accompanies this award, costing on average $192,000, Mother Teresa requested the banquet money be donated to the poor.

This action by Mother Teresa always challenges me to keep my focus and priorities on people so the applause or achievements don't undermine my core passion. If we get distracted by the accolades or projects, and miss the importance of people, we can be fairly certain that the impact and fulfillment from pursuing our dream will decline and possibly disappear.

This lesson became crystal clear to me when I changed my mindset for NightCare. My thinking began to change from speedy to slow, from numbers to nurture and from the babies and toddlers living in a nightmare to them finding love and safety in NightCare. I settled into more of a marathon mindset rather than a sprint mentality. As my mindset slowly changed and matured, our NightCare attendance began to gradually creep upward.

Little by little, every month, I watched our numbers increase and I began to frame our growth in terms of one baby and one toddler at a time. Along with the increase in nightly attendance, we learned lots of important lessons about visiting our moms in their homes, so that we became more relational and connected with them as we loved and nurtured their babies.

We also learned about the power of integrity and being transparent. These lessons came as we began to integrate some open house events into our monthly routines, inviting moms to come to our center for snacks so they could meet our nannies and tour the facility. Those open houses helped build trust and show the integrity of our heart and motive in the practical and nightly facilitation of NightCare. Most of all, being compassionate, regardless of the circumstances or events, came to be an essential mindset that we endeavor to maintain.

All of these lessons and practices helped us grow not only in the quality of our love, but also in the number of babies for whom we could provide NightCare. About 12 months later we were averaging 22 babies and toddlers in nightly attendance at our first NightCare center.

LESSONS LEARNED

PERSISTENCE

In addition to keeping a healthy focus on the right priorities, it's also helpful to grow and strengthen the persistence muscle. I learned how important it is to be persistent. Having just a handful of babies at NightCare in our first months of existence made this lesson a three-dimensional experience. I remember the disappointment I felt when I learned that only four babies had come to NightCare when we first opened. I had wrestled in my heart with feeling discouraged and even thought about quitting before I had barely begun to start!

Sometimes we can be easily discouraged when we don't see immediate results in something that we deem to be important, helpful and redemptive. I had to assess my own motives: Am I doing this to make myself feel good or am I doing this because I love and care for these babies? If my endgame is to love these babies, then I'm not going to quit before I've barely started.

I decided to stay the course and look into ways that could help us communicate to the moms how much we want to protect and look after their babies while they work. I also came to appreciate the massive significance of being steady and keeping our integrity - being true to our word, regardless of the number of babies that come or do not come.

INTEGRITY

There were many lessons for me that were a vital part of these early months and years of NightCare. In addition to persistence, it was vitally important for us to have integrity - to do what we say we will do and be who we say we are. Integrity is bolstered with transparency, so we decided to begin holding open houses to invite the moms to tour our home, meet our workers, inspect and ask questions. Over the course of the next year we did several of these open houses, in addition to going several times a week into their neighborhood, inviting the moms to leave their babies and toddlers with us at NightCare while they work.

We've integrated this open house concept into the building blocks that we now require whenever we open a new NightCare center. This has been an integral step to not only express integrity, but also facilitate trust with a new mom who is considering NightCare for her baby or toddler.

One of the practical ways that we endeavor to demonstrate integrity to our moms is that when she collects her baby or toddler in the morning after her work, her baby is clean, rested, safe and protected after having stayed the night in our NightCare center.

HUMILITY

Initially, when we opened NightCare, we thought it was important that our moms contribute to the care of their child, so we charged a nominal fee, equivalent to a nickel a day. We quickly learned that our idea to facilitate responsibility and participation in looking after their baby or toddler was backfiring. The moms weren't bringing their kids because they didn't have the minuscule fee and they were embarrassed to talk about this lack – it felt shameful to them.

Once again, I had to inspect my motives. Was I doing NightCare to train these moms to be responsible or was I doing NightCare to look after innocent babies and toddlers? If my first priority was babies and toddlers, then a nominal fee was pointless.

I learned that keeping my focus on serving and loving my little ones was far more essential than whatever possible lesson might happen for the occasional mom who might scrape together the nominal fee. I had to humble myself, admit my approach was faulty, and change our procedure.

I've come to the conclusion that in whatever area I am arrogant and lack humility, I have much to learn. As long as I hold onto my pride at the expense of humility, my ability to learn, grow, improve and make an impact is severely compromised and even wrecked.

CHAPTER 10 - DIVINE DISCONTENT

"No mother in her right mind would bring her son to this place! Get me outta here!" This is what my ten-year-old son said to me one night, as we snaked our way down an increasingly dark and cramped alley in a slum somewhere in Phnom Penh, Cambodia. The further down the narrow alleyway we stumbled in the darkness the less we could see, thereby heightening our other senses. The blackness seemed tangible and engrossing, and my son was squeezing my hand so hard that I offered to give him a piggyback ride. This was a no-go, although I could feel him weigh his fear against trying to be big and strong.

Suddenly, in the almost tangible darkness, it felt like we came into an open space because I couldn't feel anything nearby, a contrast from the claustrophobic alleyway we'd just traversed. But the darkness was so thick that we were swallowed into virtual oblivion, only able to hear people distantly mumbling in the dark, inky blackness. It was super creepy and, like my son, I wasn't keen on staying there long, even though our guides fished out a few babies from somewhere in the darkness, demonstrating the need for NightCare in this virtual nightmare.

We quickly backtracked and our guide explained that we were in the back yard of the main strip, where there were heaps more babies. Attempting to find more babies, in better lighting and probably a safer area, my son and I meandered our way down what seemed to be an abandoned railroad track in a densely populated and desperately poor neighborhood. And as we walked along the unlit railroad tracks I spotted a little girl, maybe two years old, with cute curly hair and a coy smile. She was warm and engaging, sitting on a stoop outside of what looked to be a house. She waved to us to follow her into the house.

I told my son to stay outside with my friend and that I would come and get him if I thought it was safe for him. He was more than happy to stay in the light with our friend whom we love and trust.

Here is something for your consideration: in order to do magnificent things, sometimes we have to take some risks and even explore what is unknown and possibly scary. Unfortunately, I think far too many people let fear restrict their exploration and what is unknown can become an obstacle rather than a hurdle.

There's no doubt that you and I have had some moments that have been less than pleasant, but let's allow those hardships to be instructional instead of constricting as we explore, learn and grow. If we don't learn and grow, it's likely that our world won't change because of the lack of our contribution. Of course, we should be safe and wise, but let's also branch out and take adventures that could be transformational!

Returning to the slum in Cambodia: I followed the little girl into the house, which turned out to be a large open room with lots of curtains and beds and a table at the front. In the wide open and well-lit room, a lady was putting on some of the ample supply of makeup that had been strewn across the table. A newborn was swinging in a hammock under a TV running some show in the Khmer language, and in the back corner another lady had just come out of a shower with a towel wrapped around her body.

My new two-year-old friend was giving me a tour of the house, which I quickly understood to be a miniature brothel. I could see under the curtains the legs to several beds and our translator exclaimed, "They're having sex behind these curtains! Should I open the curtains to show you?!"

I quickly declined as I didn't need to see a real-time display of the baby-making process. I was still quite shell-shocked from the brief tour and struggled to process my thoughts and feelings as I walked out the front door and back to my son at the train tracks.

Later, I learned that there was a very small room under that miniature brothel where the women would leave their young children, usually unattended, while they worked throughout the night. It was not uncommon for toddlers to meander out of the room unsupervised and walk in the dark, barefoot and barely dressed, wherever they fancied on any given night.

The little girl who was sitting on the stoop likely meandered out of that room under the brothel. That little girl, Chan Nu, has become very meaningful to me. Over the course of several years, starting with that first introduction, I've been around Chan Nu innumerable times and I've come to deeply care about her. Subsequent to meeting her that night, I learned that the baby in the house who was swinging in the hammock under the TV was Chan Nu's brother and his name is Pagna.

I also learned that her mom, Val, was a drug addict, a sex worker and had been diagnosed with AIDS. Little did I know when I met Chan Nu that first time, that she would become a part of my heart. Chan Nu was a street kid with base survival instincts and a seeming inability to bond or connect relationally.

Touring the miniature brothel was a new experience that marinated in my heart and soul for many days. It ignited in me a relentless passion to open NightCare in that very neighborhood. As I thought about this, I couldn't help but wonder how many more slums there were in Phnom Penh where NightCare would be urgently needed. Searching out new neighborhoods to expand our NightCare work is wildly exciting for me but many folk would be more scared than excited. In touring this new neighborhood for NightCare in Phnom Penh, where I met Chan Nu, I rapidly concluded that it was a living nightmare for the babies and toddlers - a perfect location for NightCare.

Even though we had one center up and running smoothly and the average attendance had grown to over twenty babies and toddlers every night, I wanted more. I had been in correspondence with our ground team in Cambodia about finding some possible new neighborhoods where NightCare could meet the most urgent needs of babies and toddlers of sex workers, and where any care for them was limited, deplorable or nonexistent.

"More" seems to be an essential word throughout the human experience. We want more time, money, conveniences, achievements, equity, etc. And I want more NightCare centers! In 2012, when I interviewed Ann to be the National Director for NightCare in Cambodia, I shared my vision to have multiple well-run centers throughout the nation, rather than just one center providing protection and care for a few dozen babies and toddlers.

When I explained this to Ann, she was entirely on board with the idea of having multiple centers. So it was no surprise to her that I was more than thrilled about our progress with our first center and eager to open our second. But sometimes, life can frustrate our desires for more.

What would you like more of in your life that would be meaningful and lasting? I have often found that the way to acquire more of what is meaningful is by doing what is uncommon, while maintaining a mindset of generosity. I have learned that if I give away what I want, this is often how my desires become fulfilled.

For example, it is strangely wonderful to walk through these slums and red-light areas, giving away smiles, hugs and love to anyone who will make eye contact with me. And when I get to express genuine love in these environments, I often leave these neighborhoods overflowing with love and compassion rather than fear and intolerance. It is important to pursue what is relevant and substantial instead of that which is frothy and superfluous.

At the same time NightCare was developing a larger footprint in Cambodia, my team in Denver, Colorado was facing a new challenge. Susan, who had been so instrumental in opening NightCare, needed to resign from her role with Saving Moses to look after an urgent family concern. I felt a heavy weight in my soul from my determination to expand NightCare, but this conflicted with the administrative deficiency created by Susan's departure.

With Susan leaving, it became clear to me that I'm not gifted with administrative abilities, regardless of how hard I try. Having me do the organization, administrative oversight and operational systems is like asking an amoeba to change into a giraffe! It really bothered me to lose Susan and I realized that I need people gifted in administration, operations, finance and more, to come alongside me. So I prayed.

At that time, a wonderful woman who had been an assistant to my mom many years earlier, expressed an interest in helping with Saving Moses. I eagerly welcomed PJ on my team, which now had two members: PJ and me. PJ has been an invaluable team member for many years with me. She has been faithful and dedicated, wholeheartedly embracing the vision for Saving Moses. And while I was incredibly grateful for PJ, I also recognized that we both needed additional skills and talents for Saving Moses, that neither of us possessed.

It's important to recognize the value of teamwork, and the role we can play on a team, because the truth is that we can do more together than we can by ourselves. For me, this lesson is often recycled in my life because I tend to be a maverick and try to do things on my own. But I've grown in this area, recognizing that it's entirely impossible to do anything magnificent without a team.

In relation to the need for more administrative support, when I prayed, God answered in the least expected way. One Saturday afternoon in my hometown of Denver, I found myself sitting across the table from a stranger, sharing a plate of grasshopper appetizers. We were at a luncheon for a mutual friend who was visiting from out of town. As we ate our grasshoppers, we introduced ourselves and made the customary small talk. Over the course of the conversation, I asked about her background, education and hobbies.

I learned that "Heidi" had just graduated with her master's degree in international business and was interested in doing humanitarian work for children overseas. "What a coincidence!" I said. "I have a wonderful teammate, PJ, who has been extremely helpful. But my administrative person for my new organization just resigned because of a family crisis. Why don't you come and work with us?"

Maybe this isn't exactly verbatim, but it's pretty close to how the conversation unfolded as I introduced myself, and Saving Moses, and explained what we were doing at that time. Additionally, I explained my desire to grow, along with my frustrations at my inabilities and deficiencies with operational support and administrative leadership.

Heidi was very interested in what I was describing but she explained that she had just signed a year-long contract to do operational support for a private school nearby. I asked if she'd consider doing some volunteer work for us. We needed some extensive research about NightCare and which countries around the world would be most suited for the vision of Saving Moses: most urgent and least available. She said she'd be open to helping PJ and me with some volunteer work once she settled into her new job, so we exchanged phone numbers and I said I'd be in contact with her.

Over the next several months, Heidi did heaps of essential research for us and we met several times to review her findings. In the early part of 2014, she asked if I was still interested in having her work full-time for Saving Moses since her contract at the school was up for renewal. I eagerly replied, "YES!" She began working for Saving Moses in July of 2014.

After only a few days in the office, she joined our team trip to Cambodia for ten days and that was a great introduction to the urgency and importance of NightCare. In my opinion, oftentimes the best way to learn new things is to jump in the deep end and that is exactly what Heidi did!

Here are Heidi's words from her first trip with NightCare as she describes talking with one of the moms:

"I remember sitting in a one-bedroom home, on a bed next to a mother who

brings her baby (less than a year) to NightCare. As she talked to us, she rocked her baby in a hammock as he struggled to fall asleep. She was so proud of her son; she insisted I take pictures of him with my phone. When I showed her the picture I took, she smiled widely with pride.

We sat with her as she told us her story. She was emotional as she recounted her recent past. She explained to us that she had been married twice but both of her husbands had left her. She is the sole provider for her family and works as a sex worker to make ends meet. In this industry, she makes very little money. Because of the industry, she is HIV positive. In sadness she said, 'I used to be beautiful, but I have lost so much weight and am so weak.'

She tenderly cared for her baby as she spoke to us. As a mom, I connected with her. You are trying to give your children more than what you were given. You want nothing but the best for them, but sometimes you can't give them the best. You pray that they don't have to live through the pain you have lived through.

She brings her child to NightCare. It gives her hope because she can put her child in a safe and nurturing environment when she works. It enables her to give her child the care and protection she wants him to have - the care that she, in and of herself, cannot provide him.

As we parted, I looked her in the eyes and told her through a translator that she is a good mother. She looked at me with a smile. In that moment, we had a connection that surpassed our cultural and language barriers. We were both mothers who loved our children and wanted to do whatever we could for them. I will always remember her and her precious baby."

I totally love that Heidi was so deeply impacted by her first trip with Saving Moses!

Both PJ and Heidi have been with Saving Moses for more than five years now and their contributions have been nothing less than totally astounding! Over the course of these years we've added four countries to our work, run multiple campaigns to save thousands of babies, added five

NightCare centers and more than fifty employees, and have tremendously expanded our work.

Teamwork is an essential ingredient to doing great things and I'm absolutely privileged to join such incredible people who are devoted to this mission of preserving life from its most fragile beginning!

When I think back to 2013, I know it was a challenging year for me in my soul because I felt a powerful drive to expand and do more, but I didn't have the finances, people resources, administrative structure or operational wisdom to expand. I had an overabundance of zeal, but an undersupply of provision. So, when Susan resigned, it added more fuel to my frustration fire. Thankfully, God often comes through to help us in unexpected ways. Meeting Heidi at a random lunch was one of God's amazing provisions!

At the same time Saving Moses was experiencing growing pains in our home office, I was also supremely discontented with the size and quantity of our NightCare work in Cambodia. Not only did I visit a very shady neighborhood with my ten-year-old son, but I also kept hearing about other red-light areas throughout Phnom Penh. Furthermore, from the research that Heidi did in her volunteer work for us, I learned of other large red-light districts around the world. My eyes were opened to the monstrous size of the sex industry, though I stayed laser-focused on the babies and toddlers who are the innocent ones.

I continued to press hard to expand our NightCare work, specifically in Cambodia because of the urgency and need I saw when I walked through the mini brothel described at the beginning of this chapter. And our team in Cambodia stepped up to the plate, worked hard and opened our second NightCare in Phnom Penh, less than eighteen months after the opening of the first center.

LESSONS LEARNED

TEAMWORK

Losing Susan drove home the poignant lesson that if there is to be any accomplishment that exceeds my passion and abilities, I must appreciate that I am merely one member of a team. To be sure, there have always been very helpful people along the journey with Saving Moses. Various people have contributed with marketing help, financial assistance, administrative wisdom, photography and video support, operational collaboration and loads more!

All of this has been extremely helpful to me at the fundamental level of recognizing the value and impact of teamwork. While the importance of teamwork may seem obvious to some, it's been a tremendous revelation for me because at my core I'm fiercely independent, which can be a weakness of crippling proportion. I've come to realize that even with my best effort, I'm entirely inadequate to accomplish anything significant or lasting on my own. I need people who are not like me, who are gifted in diverse ways, and who see things from different perspectives. As we work together, respecting each other's talents and contributions, we can accomplish astounding achievements that far exceed our individual abilities!

TRUST

Even though the word "trust" is short, easy to say and commonly verbalized, it can be a challenging verb and lesson. At the beginning of this chapter, I described a situation in which my son had to trust me even though he was super scared. And with Saving Moses, as we were beginning to get more established with NightCare and expand past our first center, I had to grow in my ability to trust not only God, but also other people.

Because I'm so independent, it's sometimes very difficult for me to trust. I have to be purposeful in choosing to trust both God and others. Now I recognize that each mom who allows us to look after her baby is trusting us with her most important treasure. Trust is an essential ingredient for accomplishing very significant goals!

It can be challenging to trust because of disappointments we've had in our past where we've been burned, betrayed or deeply hurt by people we've trusted. And sometimes it's even tricky to trust God because He is invisible, and because of disappointments, unanswered prayers and times when God may have seemed absent or disinterested. But the decision to trust is necessary for the journey with teamwork.

It's true that both God and people will disappoint us, but regardless of how we feel or the circumstances in which we find ourselves, it's nonetheless essential that we choose to trust.

CHAPTER 11 - BROADEN THE HORIZONS

A scantily clad little girl, Sreyan, maybe three years old, bounces into the open room with eager enthusiasm. She springs past the waiting toys and friendly faces and goes straight to the wash basin filled with warm water, soap, and shampoo, so she can wash off the dirt and muck from playing in her neighborhood earlier in the day. While Sreyan embraces the warm and familiar welcome of her NightCare center, her mom signs her in with the nanny at the front door, a well-practiced habit in this mom's nightly routine.

As I watch Sreyan's mom, I can see that she has mixed emotions. Her sincere smile expresses the relief and gratitude she has for not only the NightCare center, but also for the nannies who will look after her daughter, making sure she's safe, clean, well fed and has slept through the night. But I can also see her shoulders sag after she signs in her daughter and turns to go back to the street, where she will trade sex for money throughout much of the night, endeavoring to earn enough for rent, food and basic utilities. This is likely the only way she can earn a living to provide for her family.

Many people ask me, sometimes with disdain, why these women choose to work in the sex industry and why they don't get themselves out of such a deplorable situation. Whenever I answer this concern, I endeavor to pause and reply with grace and poise. No woman considers it her dream profession to have sex with multiple strange men for countless nights, months and sometimes years on end.

Ultimately, these women are often in this profession because they have no other option to earn a living. Most of them are illiterate and have no learned trade or skill, and many of them have moved long distances from their families. They hope to earn a better living in a city and leave behind farming, and a life of subsistent existence. This is not uncommon in the rural provinces of Cambodia and other similarly poor countries.

As such, human trafficking is profusely common in much of the developing world, so there are a variety of reasons these moms wind up in such dire circumstances. Many times, these women take on the most degrading profession to care for those whom they most love: their children.

Consider that when her daughter, Sreyan, joyfully bounces into the safe and familiar NightCare center, her mom is relieved and simultaneously dejected, knowing what the night in front of her will hold. Of course, I also know that not every mother is so nurturing and altruistic toward her children.

Many of the moms who bring us their babies for NightCare are addicted to drugs, suffer from mental instability, carry abusive backgrounds into their present parenting, and lack the necessary maturity and know-how to care for a baby or toddler. I've seen more than a few moms who parent in ways that could be hurtful to their child.

But from a different perspective and voice, let's take a look at what NightCare is like for our babies and toddlers. Caitlyn is a young woman who has been on a couple of our team trips over the years. She's wise, insightful and compassionate, so her thoughts and feelings about joining an evening of NightCare are very compelling. Here's what Caitlyn says about evenings in a NightCare center:

"NightCare is one of the most beautiful things that I have ever had the opportunity to be a part of. The children run in to the center, with huge smiles on their faces, to be bathed and clothed after being dropped off by mom. The moms are greeted and loved on as they drop off their babies. After being bathed, the kids have an opportunity to play with the toys in the center. This was the most magical time for me. Every single child had such a distinct personality, little friend groups that they had formed, and passions that were so unique to every individual. One of my good friends, August, came and the boys climbed all over him like a jungle gym. The girls ages 4-5 seemed to click with me the most. They had high energy like the boys, but also loved to just sit in your arms and spend quality time together. After play time they ate dinner, which the nannies had prepared before they came (the nannies are also the most wonderful women you will ever meet). The little ones sit in a circle with their food and they have a communal dinner. I really loved participating in this because kids ages 0–5 would all sit in this circle and just break bread together. After dinner, we had circle time, which is so sweet. The kids gather together in a circle and practice being quiet, being patient, cooperative, and other essential life skills. They sing songs together, dance together, and pray together. It is really amazing to watch the kids take authority and step out to sing the song alone. The shyest kids feel so comfortable that they are able to stand in front of their peers and lead them. NightCare really nurtures these kids to be outstanding individuals."

In contrast to Caitlyn's observations, consider the answer one of our moms gave when we implored her to let her daughter come to NightCare. "No, I won't let my three-year-old daughter go to NightCare because she helps me earn a living by selling condoms to my clients. But you're welcome to look after Pagna, her little brother." This was one of many conversations with Val, the drug-addicted mother to Chan Nu and Pagna, whom I wrote about in the last chapter.

There have been innumerable times when various members of the Saving Moses team have pleaded with Val on behalf of her daughter. We've offered her weekly food, transportation help and various resources to cajole her into letting Chan Nu come to NightCare. And there were many times I showed up at Val's door and begged her to let us look after Chan Nu while she worked. It wasn't uncommon for Val to be drugged out of her mind, stumbling through a stupor-filled dialogue of nonsense and incoherence. And there was Chan Nu, day after day, living in squalor, dysfunction, danger and sheer depravity.

Now, several years later, Val is dead, either from her drug addiction or AIDS, which she passed along to her son, Pagna. Tragically, Pagna went missing when he was about two years old. No one in the neighborhood knew where he was.

When I asked Chan Nu if she missed her brother, her eyes became sad and she quietly nodded her head. And when I asked Chan Nu if she missed her mom, shortly after she died, she gave me a blank look, unphased and detached. She mechanically answered with appropriate words, but the absence of emotion and expression left me questioning the substance of any mother and daughter connection. Chan Nu has since been adopted by another mother in the neighborhood and I've had some dialogue with her new mom.

I'm not convinced in my soul that Chan Nu is doing well. And it's difficult to know how much Chan Nu says is true because lying and deception have been integral ingredients to her daily survival. Such lying is further enhanced by her mindset of distrust that was baked into her survival from infancy.

As much as I want to tell you that the moms of our babies and toddlers are benevolent, nurturing and maternal, that's not always true. In my years of doing NightCare, I've met a wide spectrum of moms whose babies and toddlers we care for every night. Some moms seem like angels and other moms, not so much. But regardless of who a mom is or is not, her baby or toddler needs genuine love, attention, food, nurture and protection.

If I let myself get sidetracked with the depravity and dysfunction of a mom, I'll miss investing in the immediate and urgent need in front of me. This is a baby who has fallen asleep on my shoulder. Or a toddler who is demanding my attention. And the little one leaning against me who has been roughed up from a bad day, week or month, watching with timid attention as others play.

In relation to these moms, I remind myself that there are many organizations that are making an impact with them through vocational assistance, counseling, training, etc. Just because a baby or toddler isn't able to clearly communicate their desires, thoughts or what happens to them on a daily basis, doesn't mean that they don't need or crave genuine love. And many times, that toddler who is violent and loud, or the baby who cries unconsolably, is communicating the nightmare in which they live every day.

With all that being said, after the happenchance meeting of Chan Nu on the stoop of the mini brothel, I became intensely passionate to open our second NightCare. I met Chan Nu in July of 2013 and we opened our second NightCare in Chan Nu's neighborhood about six months later. This means that in six months, not only did we keep our first NightCare center operating almost every day, we also located a rental house close to Chan Nu's neighborhood, cleaned and prepared it, hired a facility manager along with nannies, and went into the neighborhood multiple times to invite the moms to bring their babies and toddlers to NightCare.

Again, we faced huge hurdles with our second location, similar to what we faced on our first go-around with opening NightCare. Thankfully, this time we didn't have quite as steep of a learning curve as we had with our first center.

Within eighteen months of opening our first NightCare we had opened the second one, and I was thoroughly excited! And since we were in expansion mode, I pushed to open a third NightCare center in 2014, such that in two years we had three centers up and running six nights a week. By the end of 2014, our three NightCare centers were taking care of an average of 37 babies and toddlers on any given night.

The same year that Heidi joined the Saving Moses team, I visited Kolkata again, hoping to find some traction for NightCare. In the summer of 2014, Jody and I made our second visit to Kolkata, as she had some friends and connections there that looked promising for opening NightCare. We made a brief trip to this city, maybe three days in total, and we visited three red-light districts: Bowbazar, Kalighat and Sonagachi. We walked through all three of these neighborhoods in the daytime and I gained an even deeper appreciation for the need and importance of NightCare in these red-light districts.

I'll never forget walking through Sonagachi and thinking of the documentary I'd watched, *Born Into Brothels*, that started this incredible adventure. It was a surreal experience that became laser sharp as I heard distant voices of playful toddlers wafting through the alleyways. This beautiful sound caught my attention and I stopped my friends for a moment. "Hold up and listen! What do you hear?" They heard the same thing and we quickly followed the little voices to a place with a sign communicating some kind of daycare center, as I could vaguely deduce.

I was wildly excited to find this unexpected oasis in Sonagachi and asked loads of questions with excited anticipation and hopeful expectation. My hopeful heart always seems to get ahead of my practical brain.

The short story is that this room was used in lots of different ways throughout the week and we just happened to stumble upon it during its usage as a semi-daycare. The other functions of the room during the week included a community training center, a meeting place for a social club, storage space for some plastic gadgets and a quiet room for reflection, to name a few.

Of course, I began to imagine using that space for NightCare, and I asked a few indirect questions about the availability of the space in the evenings and throughout the night. Our hosts understood the backdrop for my questions and after some exchanges with the person in charge of that room, we learned that there was another person who owned the room and that perhaps we could contact them to enquire about its availability.

I quickly surmised that nothing in developing world red-light districts is as it seems. The reality is that the people who run the show don't readily reveal themselves, nor their power. Furthermore, the only transactions that are relatively transparent are the immediate and daily exchanges that happen between clients and sex workers. Everything beyond that is cloaked in layers of opaque administration and deflected conversations.

This resulted in lots of effort and education for me but no progress during that trip. It could have been easy to get lost in a myriad of rabbit trails and distractions if I didn't endeavor to keep my eyes on the prize of NightCare for babies and toddlers.

In addition to visiting Sonagachi for some hours, we were also able to visit during the day the red-light districts of Kalighat and Bowbazar, and again I was awestruck as I walked through those districts. While visiting Kalighat, I learned that there is a temple for the Hindu goddess, Kali, in this neighborhood, and that Kali is the regional goddess for Kolkata, formerly known as Calcutta. Immediately adjacent to the Kali Temple is the Home for the Dying, which Mother Teresa founded in 1952. As we walked around Kalighat, I became keenly aware of how the profession of sex worker is interwoven into the long history and fabric of this neighborhood. On that afternoon, I saw toddlers and kids of all ages playing in the streets. I couldn't help but wonder about what happens to them at night, and what their future will be like.

When we visited Bowbazar, in contrast, I saw only a handful of babies, perched on the hips of their moms, and my walk through that neighborhood was very disturbing to me. Even during the daytime, it was easy to see the women who were trolling for work in both Sonagachi and Bowbazar.

As we meandered through the very narrow alleyways between buildings in Bowbazar, it was like being in a maze. It felt like the tight walls were about to swallow me into their dark confines. As I walked through the slender lanes, I noticed various women standing in the doorways and looking out through the windows, both at eye-level and from the windows on the second floor. I needed to watch my step since the walkway was filled with trash, and I was again assaulted by a stench that seemed more pervasive here than it had been in the other red-light districts.

What haunts me to this day is how I felt when I looked into the eyes of the women in Bowbazar. Regardless of whatever red-light district I walk through in any country, it is my instinct to smile and look people in the eyes. Sometimes these eyes look back at me with a smile, and often the eyes express curiosity as they wonder, "What's this big foreign woman doing walking through our neighborhood?" It's also very common for me to look into the eyes of these women and get an empty and blank stare, devoid of life or interaction.

In Bowbazar, however, the eyes of the women were hostile, aggressive and defiant. In their eyes I saw violence, and a repeated warning not to trespass in that neighborhood with any attempt to bring hope, genuine love or life. It felt like the longer I walked around the more likely it was that I would be physically assaulted, since every eye that looked back at me seemed menacing. Needless to say, I breathed a deep sigh of relief when we popped out a narrow alleyway onto a main thoroughfare with fresh air.

Over the course of many years, I've walked through lots of brothels, red-light districts and shady neighborhoods. While I can appreciate the need for basic safety, I've also come to see that each person in these places wants genuine love, regardless of what their eyes say and no matter what their body language conveys. I'm also thoroughly convinced that perfect love casts out fear.

Consequently, when I decide to interact from a heart of genuine love, I'm decreasingly aware of fear until it disappears from my thoughts and feelings. I become eager to smile and be gracious, warm and welcoming with whomever I get to meet or see. No doubt, I don't always get a reciprocal smile or welcoming eyes, but genuine love is the decision I choose to make, with each step and person I see.

Going to Kolkata again was a poignant reminder about the need for NightCare in India. It helped fuel my energy and commitment to expand NightCare to that nation.

Additionally, the one-to-one interactions with Chan Nu and her mom helped ignite this fire in me to honor and value the life of one little girl. Centers, programs, logistics, administration, payroll, legal compliance and loads more, can sometimes distract us from the little girl who needs NightCare as an alternative to selling condoms to her mom's clients every night.

LESSONS LEARNED

HEARTBREAK

Nobody likes heartbreak; full stop. We avoid it, insulate ourselves from it and do everything we can to keep it on a distant planet so that we don't experience it in any way. And that's all very understandable. However, heartbreak is sometimes the catalyst that launches us into action, combating a tragedy or crusading against an injustice. Being around Chan Nu year after year is an exercise in heartbreak for me. I know that I could avoid her, and she wouldn't miss a beat. But the breaking of my heart every time I see her, and the pain I feel, fuel my passion to expand NightCare.

I think it is supremely important that we consider what breaks our heart. When we take inventory of such heartbreaks, we can allow that passion to be converted to something constructive and beneficial to the world in which we live. Perhaps it would be helpful, with God's direction and grace, to see heartbreak in terms of potential instead of avoidance.

OPTIMISM

The depravity of the daily existence of our babies and toddlers who attend NightCare can become overwhelming, and if we are not careful, debilitating. Watching a toddler stroll into our NightCare center with fresh cigarette burns or dazed from the neglect he experienced from the day, can be draining from my perspective. On the flip side, I can choose to see the potential and life that is possible for each of these babies and toddlers. No doubt there are dangers in denying the daily realities of our babies that attend NightCare, however, the future is yet to be written, and we get a chance every night to invest in possibility instead of depravity.

If we are ever going to make a difference and a positive contribution with our lives, we must live from a place of potential, optimism and hope. In contrast, being pessimistic and hopeless is a dead end. There will be no change or improvement if we do not make the daily choice to be optimistic and hopeful!

CHAPTER 12 - BANGING ON A DIFFERENT DOOR

"I have witnessed a range of human despair in my life – looked into the eyes of the homeless or mother of four who can't afford to feed her little ones. However, there's something so different about looking into the empty eyes of a three-year-old who has grown up in a brothel. Many of these babies and toddlers have endured abuse from their mothers' clients, are in the room all night long, or wandering alone in the brothel at night. The vacant-looking stare of a little one is something you can't unsee. It's hard to rationalize the muck and mire of the world we live in. But my heart repeats the celebration of NightCare. Every night, little ones are offered love, protection and innocence."

This is what my friend Emily said when I asked about her observations and feelings from visiting and working in our NightCare centers. I share her words with you because they reflect some of my passion and zeal to continue growing and expanding our NightCare work. Sometimes their eyes haunt me for months after one of my routine visits to Cambodia.

I also began to think about brothels in other countries in the developing world; not just in Cambodia or India. So, you can imagine my surprise when I heard these words from my friends:

"We didn't see an urgent need, nor overwhelming demand for NightCare in that brothel." These are the words from the team we sent to some red-light districts in Brazil in 2015. Heidi and some wise colleagues went to research and explore firsthand the real time and day-to-day living for the babies and toddlers of sex workers in the large brothels of Brazil.

I had heard of some very sizable brothels in Brazil, and based on the stories I heard, with the numbers of sex workers in the brothels, I was entirely convinced that NightCare was essential for those Brazilian red-light districts. Furthermore, Heidi's research on sex workers in the developing world substantiated that Brazil has a high quantity of sex workers, so we presumed that meant there would also be a huge need for NightCare.

Despite our extensive research and abundant statistical information, there's no substitute for boots on the ground training and education. This is precisely why it's important to go and see things firsthand, to absorb the day-to-day realities of the babies and toddlers of sex workers in these various countries.

From Heidi's stay in Brazil, we learned that this extremely large brothel had almost no babies and toddlers onsite - and I was stunned! Heidi explained to me that even though all of the moms lived in the brothel most of the time, they kept their permanent residence in the distant provinces where they left their babies and toddlers. As often as they could, the moms would make short visits back to their more permanent homes to take money to their families and spend a day or two with their children, who were far removed from their mom's brothel existence.

When Heidi described how this arrangement worked in Brazil, I was more than a little surprised because I had assumed that babies and moms stayed together, regardless of where a mom worked and regardless of what kind of work she did. I was also relieved to learn that those Brazilian sex workers had figured out a way to keep their children shielded from the horrors and atrocities that accompany the normal existence of babies and toddlers living in a brothel. As such, we made the obvious decision not to expand our NightCare work into Brazil at that time.

Regardless of what we learned in Brazil, expansion is always in my heart because I feel God's compassion and love for the babies and toddlers. I say this because of what it says in Jeremiah 22:16, *"'He pled the cause of the afflicted and needy; Then it was well. Is not that what it means to know Me?' Declares the LORD."* From my perspective, I can't think of a needier and more afflicted portion of humanity than babies and toddlers of sex workers in the developing world. And the more I do to help these tiny treasures, the better it is for my soul - and the more intimately I know the Creator of the Universe.

That outcome in Brazil helped me to appreciate the immense diversity of the existence of sex workers in the red-light slums of the developing world. At the same time, I'm very grateful that our NightCare efforts in Cambodia have continued to expand, such that by July of 2015 we opened our fourth NightCare center in Phnom Penh. Considering that we opened our very first NightCare center in the first half of 2012, I'm positively thrilled that we had been able to open four NightCare centers in three years.

By the end of 2015, we were averaging approximately 55 babies and toddlers in all four of our NightCare centers. Although 55 babies and toddlers may not seem like a large number based on the enormity of the need, this was a tremendous success considering how inexperienced we were at that time. Furthermore, when I think about what it takes to keep a NightCare center up and running, multiplied by four, I'm still in awe at the immensity of what was accomplished in such a short amount of time.

Each NightCare center requires no less than three workers, and more often requires up to seven nannies to look after our babies during the evening and throughout the night. Additionally, each center needs to be kept clean, supplies must be purchased regularly (food, laundry detergent, soap, etc.) and security must be provided, since this is a premium priority given our locations in dangerous neighborhoods.

To help cultivate trust with the moms who are sex workers, we also continue to facilitate the open houses to welcome potential moms, along with conducting community outreaches several times a month. In addition, we maintain high child protection vigilance and oversee the nightly check-in system for each child, along with facility maintenance, repairs, legal reporting and compliance, and a plethora of additional responsibilities.

It is no small feat to keep one NightCare center operating smoothly. It is incredibly powerful then to consider that we had four centers opened and running within the course of three years. By the end of 2015, we had more than twenty employees in Cambodia alone.

When you think about having four NightCare centers operational in such a short time, it's helpful to keep the reason for NightCare as the central focus. The reason we do NightCare is because of the need to protect, nurture and love babies and toddlers of sex workers at the most vulnerable time of day for those little ones. Let me share a story of one of our babies to help us keep the urgent needs of these babies in laser-sharp focus.

Consider Chanda, who was born in Phnom Penh a few years ago. Chanda's mom is a sex worker who lives in a slum over a sewage river. She's reluctant to leave Chanda with any neighbors when she is doing her nighttime job because many of them have molested other little girls in the slum. Chanda's mom wants to protect her! Before NightCare, Chanda was at risk every night that her mother was away at work. And every night her mom stayed home there was a shortage of food. I find that to be a deplorable choice: food or safety!

When NightCare opened, Chanda's mom began bringing her every night. Consequently, both Chanda and her mom are relieved that she is receiving genuine love, nurturing care, protection, healthy dinners and safe sleep. Are there other concerns and issues for Chanda's mom that need to be addressed and resolved? Absolutely. But the urgent need to protect and look after Chanda at nighttime has been met, and this is a tremendous relief to Chanda's mom!

Here's what my friend Joe says about watching the impact of NightCare over the course of several years:

"After spending time in the neighborhoods during the day, and meeting several of the babies and toddlers who go to NightCare, I have seen such a transition in their countenance and behavior. I've seen the progression of this transformation year after year on return trips. I've also seen the impact of this on the moms. This experience has led some of them to seek out alternative employment to better their lives."

Joe's observations express why I am driven to open more NightCare centers. I am desperate to see these babies receiving genuine love, enjoying a healthy meal and sleeping in a safe place. So, in my mind, more centers equal more safe babies! Thanks to Heidi's wisdom and teamwork, we began to think more strategically about expanding NightCare.

I'm so very thankful for Heidi because she's both strategic and purposeful in how she approaches problems and makes decisions. Her influence has helped me to be less impulsive and significantly more effective. The more NightCare centers we opened; the more Heidi recognized the need to strengthen our administrative oversight.

We needed to be sure that we were in legal compliance with the laws and regulations of Cambodia, in addition to doing payroll, annual reviews for our nannies, monthly accounting, rental contracts, etc. In order to meet the needs of our growing work, we hired an Administrative Director in Cambodia, Narith. Bringing Narith on board freed our facility managers from heavy administrative responsibilities. In turn, they were better able to work with the nannies in each center to ensure that our babies and toddlers consistently receive proper care and attention.

Shortly after Narith joined Saving Moses, and after some enlightening conversations with my team, I came to understand that I needed to put my passion to expand on pause - not stop; just pause. My team explained to me that we needed to consolidate our efforts to fill our existing centers before we added more centers. I am so very grateful for their input!

As I began to reflect on this, I came to see the wisdom of adjusting my focus so that our team could maximize our existing resources and get the most out of our current centers. They were essentially telling me that we didn't have the capacity to both fill our current centers with babies and toddlers, and increase the number of centers we had at the same time.

It took me some time to sit with their advice and wisdom, maybe because I'm so passionate to make this essential, nightly intervention available to as many babies as possible! So, hearing that I needed to pause for a season so that we could fill our existing centers was initially difficult for me to embrace.

After some reflection, I agreed with their wisdom and temporarily restrained my expansion passion so our teams could concentrate on maximizing the centers that were open at that time.

When we began to focus on filling our existing centers, we started to see the number of babies and toddlers in attendance increase. When we were in the mode to increase the number of centers we were opening, we averaged between 10-15 babies and toddlers in each center, for a total of approximately 50 babies and toddlers per night. When I let our teams focus on filling our existing centers, our average attendance jumped up by almost ten babies and toddlers per center.

We began concentrating on walking through our neighborhoods to meet more moms with increasing consistency. We increased the number of open houses we hosted for our moms, and we were more purposeful to follow up with moms when we didn't see their baby or toddler after a few nights.

As a result of these efforts, each center was averaging more than 20 babies every night, making the total combined nightly average for all of our centers more than 80 babies and toddlers! I'm extremely grateful to our team for being so thoughtful and strategic with our resources and helping me to see their wisdom! I'm also grateful that they are patient with me, letting me grow and learn alongside them, as we work together to express genuine love to the least of the least!

At the same time that I agreed to put my expansion passion on pause, I became even more intent on seeing our NightCare centers become as effective as possible. For this reason, I'll never forget asking my tuk-tuk driver to take me to Chan Nu's neighborhood on the last evening of one of my trips to Cambodia. On that particular trip I had learned that Chan Nu's mom, before she died, was again not letting her daughter attend our NightCare, in the undulating cycle of letting her come and not letting her come.

Our team had visited Chan Nu's mom many times, offering to give her rice, vegetables, meat, cooking oil, etc. in exchange for letting Chan Nu come to NightCare. My heart was broken on this trip, because Chan Nu's mom adamantly refused to let her come to NightCare. Before I caught my plane home that night, I decided to make my last stop on my way to the airport a pleading visit to Chan Nu's mom, asking her to please let her daughter attend NightCare.

This gut-wrenching visit still affects me. As we drove up to the train tracks across from the alleyway where Chan Nu and her mom lived, Chan Nu was sitting on the tracks as the shadows increased and the light dwindled with the setting of the sun. It was already past 6:30p.m., and Chan Nu was playing unsupervised around the train tracks. Through my tuk-tuk driver I asked about her day, what she was doing, where her brother was and where I could find her mom.

Chan Nu replied with her normal coy and elusive answers, and I deduced that her mom was at home a few steps down the alleyway and maybe getting ready for the evening. I risked going down the alleyway by myself, even though it was getting dark, because my heart was breaking for Chan Nu to be allowed to come to NightCare. When I got to the ladder that led to the open wooden platform where Chan Nu's mom lived, I gingerly ambled up a few rungs and called for Chan Nu's mom with my limited Khmer language skills. As I peeked over the ladder, I saw a messy floor strewn with clothes, pots and pans, fish bones, flies, a mattress, etc. As my eyes adjusted to the dim light, I saw Chan Nu's mom and I gave her a friendly Khmer greeting. I said her daughter's name and motioned for her to come with me as I also said NightCare.

I could tell that Chan Nu's mom was high on drugs as I tried to communicate with her, but I also knew that she understood what I was asking, since I'd already met her several times during previous visits. Furthermore, I'm the large Caucasian woman who traipses around her neighborhood from time to time, and I knew that we had previously begged her to let Chan Nu come to NightCare. So my efforts were merely an attempt to add a different verse to the same song.

I was hopeful that her maternal heart would soften toward her daughter and she would let us look after Chan Nu in NightCare. She shook her head "no" and I pleaded with her with my eyes, the tone of my voice, and my body language. But she wouldn't be persuaded. Despite my efforts and the intensity of my emotions, Chan Nu would not be allowed to attend NightCare that night, and I was extremely disturbed.

I returned to my tuk-tuk by the train tracks, near Chan Nu, and I sat there with my driver. I seriously considered just scooping up Chan Nu and taking her to NightCare before I left for the airport. As I thought about it, I concluded that I could be arrested for possible child abduction and that wouldn't be helpful. My only option was to leave Chan Nu by the train tracks that night because her mom wouldn't give me permission to take her to NightCare.

I sat in my tuk-tuk a few minutes longer and watched Chan Nu. Although she was young by her number of years, she unfortunately was not innocent for her age. She was sucking on a lollipop and through my driver I asked about her little brother. She replied that he was at NightCare. When I asked if she'd like to go to NightCare she didn't give a direct answer. Instead, she looked the other way and took a deep breath. Then she got up and picked her way through the debris, rocks and ruts, down the alleyway, I supposed to her home. There was nothing more that I could do at that point.

The sun had gone down and it was getting darker by the minute. I was the only Caucasian person in a very unsafe neighborhood. I don't speak the Khmer language, and I didn't want to put my tuk-tuk driver at risk. I was at a dead end, and my only option was to give up for the night and drive to the airport to catch my flight back to Denver. I cried with a heavy heart as we drove away from the train tracks.

The gravity of that night never leaves me, and now, years later, my heart still feels heavy and despondent. Obviously, Chan Nu didn't attend NightCare that night and she was only allowed by her mom to come sporadically over the course of time.

At this point, Chan Nu is now beyond the age of attending NightCare, as we limit our care to the ages of 0-5. Since she's now older than five, what does she do? That's a great question! Thankfully, there are a number of well-run organizations that specifically care for the needs of children over the age of five, and Saving Moses is privileged to partner with some of those organizations to ensure that children like Chan Nu are protected.

LESSONS LEARNED

ZEAL BALANCED WITH WISDOM

When it comes to NightCare, I have no shortage of zeal, and it doesn't take very much to get me amped up on the subject! I'm zealous because I know the real-life horrors many babies and toddlers endure every night when NightCare isn't available.

Some of the horror stories include a toddler that almost drowned from a water tank, which tipped over in the room where he was locked in by himself while his mom worked. I've heard of babies being drugged and put under beds so they don't interfere with their moms work on the bed. And I've heard of an "uncle" looking after a female toddler; when her mom returned from her nighttime sex work, her toddler daughter was bleeding from her private area. These stories and many others cause me to be exceptionally zealous on their behalf.

Balancing my zeal with practical wisdom has been an extremely valuable lesson that I continue to learn, even as I write this. Zeal that is harnessed to wisdom is a synergistic combination that can create astounding changes and revolution. I'm very grateful for this lesson!

VERIFY BEFORE IMPLEMENTING

There have been countless times when I've been absolutely certain that my thinking and assumptions were correct, only to learn upon greater inspection that I was absolutely wrong. Brazil was an extremely helpful lesson for me in this regard. I was convinced that because the number of sex workers in the large brothel in Brazil was so high, the need for NightCare was indisputable. And I couldn't have been more wrong! There is good value in a gut feeling, but nothing can replace the actual verification that comes from an onsite visit.

Never let the implementation process come before the verification exercise. As one of my friends says, "Look and then leap; aim and then shoot." Leaping and shooting without looking and aiming can be wasteful and ineffective, if not destructive and lethal.

CHAPTER 13 – A STEP BACK AND TWO FORWARD!

On one of my visits to Phnom Penh, in the middle of the day, Heidi and I were walking around one of the city's most famous landmarks. The area was replete with tourists, and languid sex workers trolling for possible day clients. As we were about to leave the area, a man walked up to Heidi and me, speaking in Khmer. He pointed to a lawn chair behind him, just off the sidewalk and under a tree. On the lawn chair I saw a dirty, crumpled up, men's dress shirt that started to move. And then someone peeked out from under the ragged shirt!

That was when I saw her; a little girl, looking out from under the shirt, and I was very perplexed. I wondered what the guy was doing and immediately became hyper suspicious. *"What was this guy trying to do in the middle of the day?"* I thought as I slowed my pace. When we walked closer, the man pulled back the shirt to show me who I could buy, or possibly help. He said a number in English that sounded like four dollars, as I instinctively shook my head, "No." Immediately, he cut the price in half and I was shocked!

I tried to take in the frail victim with my eyes. Maybe she was four or five years old, with ratty hair, matted and twiggy, and eyes glazed and hazy, vacant but for pain and fear. When I looked into her eyes, nothing returned my gaze, and a myriad of thoughts, questions and emotions flooded into my soul. "Who is this little girl? What had happened to her to leave her lying on a lawn chair, haphazardly covered? Was she being offered for sale to any likely customer? Was the man asking for money to help this little girl? If so, why did he lower the amount of money for assistance? If the man was offering to sell her, where could I find a policeman to arrest him for what was certain to be human trafficking?" These were some of the thoughts and questions pouring through my mind as we climbed into our tuk-tuk. Heidi and I were totally blown away.

In the tuk-tuk, we talked about this little girl, helping her, and the possibility of buying her to rescue her from such a depraved existence. We quickly concluded that if we gave the man some money to help her, there would be no way to verify that he would use the money for what we intended. If we were to buy her, we would be guilty of trafficking. We tried to come up with alternative ideas and solutions, but we concluded that there was nothing we could immediately do. The rest of that tuk-tuk ride was quiet as we each sat with our thoughts and emotions, uncomfortable, angry, distraught, and vehemently outraged.

As we rode away in our tuk-tuk, I pondered how it would go over with my husband if I had bought that little girl, to rescue her. "Guess what, Reece! I bought her at a half-price discount, only two dollars! I gave her a bath so now she smells nice, and I'm sure her eyes will turn on one day, hopefully."

Of course, I couldn't buy the little girl, even though I would have the best of intentions. Buying humans is illegal, even when one's motives are pure and altruistic. But this was another sobering wake-up call to us about the urgent need for NightCare, even though that unforgettable incident took place in the middle of the day. It still shatters me, even as I write about it for you now, almost four years later.

That encounter wasn't a part of my normal, daily grid; not even in all of my travels and my work with NightCare. Our moms don't drop off their babies and ask for payment, like the man in the park offering to sell us that little girl. In contrast, our moms fully expect to collect their babies in the morning, after they have been washed, loved, fed, snuggled and have slept safe and secure.

But that little four-year-old girl was huddled on a lawn chair, hidden under a shirt and up for sale. When Heidi and I replied negatively, the vendor cut his price in half and we quickly moved away, perplexed in the moment and infuriated when we came to understand what had transpired.

It's often these unexpected moments that capture my attention and interrupt the mundane. Just when I am feeling comfortable, and like I'm making headway and doing good work, something like being asked to buy a little girl, in the middle of the day at a public park, vandalizes my normal and leaves me emotionally wrecked. These grave moments also serve to add fuel to passion, attention to focus, determination to decisions and intensity to urgent.

It's not surprising that I returned home from that trip in July with renewed zeal to expand our NightCare work over the course of the rest of that year! For the remaining months, we stayed steady with our NightCare work in Cambodia, and I continued to advocate for further expansion. But there was a glitch that caught me by surprise. As we flipped the page on the calendar to begin a new year in 2016, little did I know that it would be one of the hardest years of my life.

In the first few months of the year, we visited India again and explored a new city, in addition to going back to Kolkata for a quick visit. We visited more red-light districts and met people who were trying to make daily living in those areas more bearable, primarily for the sex workers. My main reason for making the trip was to once again look into opening NightCare in that nation, hopefully in 2016.

I wanted to check out the areas more and hopefully meet people with whom we might align for the possibility of doing NightCare together. During our two-city visit, we went through several red-light districts and met with a handful of wonderful people to discuss opening NightCare in India.

Sadly, nothing permanent resulted from that trip. Sometimes I feel like India is the door in the hallway that stays locked so that I'll see if there's another doorknob that's more receptive. While this can be very frustrating, I've also come to appreciate the importance of God's direction even when it's a closed door, possibly waiting for better timing and more suitable partnerships.

By this point in our journey with NightCare, at our home base in Denver, we had done some extensive research and analysis on the developing world, in order to identify and qualify where the needs for NightCare had the greatest demand. To accomplish this, our team created a matrix with several evaluation factors that were weighted in varying degrees of importance. Some of these factors included:

- The quantity of sex workers in a country

- The legal posture of a nation in relation to the sex industry

- NGO's/non-profits currently working in that country within the industry

- Risk and danger potential in that country

- Financial outlay/requirements to start up and maintain NightCare on an annual basis

This matrix gave us a framework to discover not only the areas with the most urgent and greatest need for NightCare, but it also gave us a more realistic perspective on what would be required to open and sustain NightCare in these countries. Our team did a thoroughly magnificent job acquiring the data to plug into this matrix, and there were very robust and thoughtful conversations. All of this facilitated a well-defined and carefully selected list for our targeted efforts to introduce and open NightCare across the developing world.

On a personal level, this exercise forced me to be less impulsive, and allowed my very intelligent and highly motivated team to get their arms around doing NightCare in alignment with a cohesive strategy. This was a valuable upgrade to my zealous but impetuous instincts, which could possibly dilute our attention and efforts with seemingly urgent diversions. Not surprisingly, it's very difficult for me to hear of or see an urgent need for NightCare and not immediately gather all my passions and resources to focus on meeting such a need.

When I agreed to participate in our matrix operation, I began to see the wisdom of using information and strategy to direct and organize our efforts, rather than subjecting our efforts to my impulsive reactions. My team helps me to be more effective, and our passionate dedication fuels us to be effective on a long-term basis, rather than a short-term transaction.

This is exactly what babies and toddlers need most in their desperate situations: long-term commitment, attentive care and steady nurture. While a one-time deposit of care into a needy situation is helpful on a limited basis, our commitment to keeping NightCare available on a continual basis is what makes the sustained and lasting difference for each baby and toddler. Genuine love is not merely a one-time transaction.

For Saving Moses to be effective, it is critical to our mission and vision that we keep our focus on babies and toddlers. Here are some observations from Morgan about the impact of NightCare on a brother and sister that attend NightCare:

"I have a hard time putting into words the change I see in the lives of the babies. After all, they are five and won't remember most of the times spent in NightCare. But there was this one girl who was four that I met in the neighborhood, and there she was being a mom to her little brother. She took care of him all day because her parents wouldn't. But when she came into NightCare, she became a four-year-old. She was able to laugh and play and just be a kid for the night, without worrying about her brother. Without NightCare, she would never have the opportunity to be a child. She would never know what it feels like to be loved. Even if the memories of nights fade, love remains. Love makes a difference and brings hope into the lives of the babies."

Morgan's words beautifully capture the stark contrasts between the grim but daily realities for this older sister juxtaposed with her young age and playful heart. This is a beautiful example of why I am so passionate to expand NightCare, even though our trip to India didn't yield any immediate progress. As the weeks passed and turned into months, it became increasingly clear that again, I wouldn't be able to open NightCare in India any time in the near future.

We continued to follow up on the face-to-face conversations we had in country, but we encountered many obstacles to opening NightCare there. Some of those obstacles included dropped communications, location uncertainties and changing priorities for the local NGO's working in the various red-light districts. As a result, many men and women whom I had met and were working in humanitarian contexts, had decided to move back to their home countries. The weeks turned into months, and I found myself again at the locked door of NightCare in India.

Suddenly, my focus on India was interrupted by a personal crisis. At the beginning of April, we took a family vacation over Spring Break at a local ski resort in Colorado. During our vacation, I had a snowboarding accident that left me hazy and dazed for a very long time. The short story is that I accidentally did a backflip while flying super-fast down a ski run. I landed on my head and sustained a relatively severe concussion, even though I had been wearing a helmet.

As I look back on this injury, I probably could have shortened my recovery time if I had been less stubborn. This means that I didn't go to the doctor until a week after the accident and, in general, I didn't invest the proper rest and care necessary for a timely recovery.

Consequently, it took what seemed an eternity to me to properly recover from the concussion, and the rest of 2016 was a very challenging year for me. Some things that I struggled with during my recovery included memory loss, cognitive gaps where I couldn't understand complicated conversations, mental fatigue, emotional volatility and large quantities of frustration and impatience.

Thankfully, our team in Cambodia was fully engaged with filling our four NightCare centers, so there wasn't any capacity to facilitate opening a new center in Cambodia for that year. But even with that said, I'm still hardwired to expand NightCare, such that it's very instinctual for me to look for new opportunities, even when I'm injured and not able to think clearly or operate at full capacity.

During our annual team trip for NightCare in Cambodia, I took a few of my friends to a potential neighborhood for a future NightCare location. This neighborhood was a famous apartment complex called "Boding." [1] This large apartment complex was built in the early 1960s under the leadership of King Sihanouk, and over the course of time it became dilapidated and very shady. Even in the daytime, when we wandered the dank hallways of the complex, it felt like we were walking through a real-life horror story.

When we walked through that extensive complex in 2016, the unlit hallways were overrun with trash, rank with refuse and more than a little dangerous. What still lingers in my memory from our visit is the image of a whimpering baby, swinging in a makeshift hammock. She was in an open-air stairwell, and her drug-dazed mom was knocked out nearby, catatonic and almost unresponsive.

As I absorbed that scene with my eyes and my heart, I felt an urgency to set up NightCare in that neighborhood, particularly as I later heard outrageous stories about the routine evening escapades that were taking place in and around that building.

While there were upstanding and honest citizens endeavoring to eke out a day-to-day existence there, it was nevertheless teeming with illegal activities, and it was a thoroughly unsafe place to raise babies and toddlers.

Even though my brain was injured from the concussion, my heart was still deeply moved and touched by my time in Boding. How can a person see an innocent baby swinging in a hammock, accessible to any malicious intent, and not be deeply affected at a primordial level? But when I processed the

---

[1] *https://www.phnompenhpost.com/national-post-depth/lights-out-white-building-residents*

situation, I still had to acknowledge the immediate and ongoing priority of our local team - to fill our current NightCare centers before opening more.

I'm grateful that our team in Cambodia was completely engrossed in the initiative to fill our existing centers rather than opening a new center around Boding. I say this because that particular apartment complex was torn down the following year, as a result of its dilapidated condition. The plan is to replace it with a more modern high-rise apartment building.

Looking back on my attempt to access Boding taught me another important lesson about being an NGO engaged in providing humanitarian assistance to babies and toddlers, whose mothers work in the sex industry. The lesson is that virtually nothing is permanent in this industry, except for the basic transactions and continuous results: people pay for sex. The outcomes of those transactions are varied but often include an increase in the number of babies born.

While our team in Cambodia was totally focused on filling our current NightCare centers, the team at our home base in Denver was seriously engaged in researching the opportunities for opening NightCare in new countries. We narrowed our scope to five main countries based on extensive research and analysis, and the country that seemed to be most available to us at that time was Bangladesh.

As we were looking at making NightCare available in different countries, and specifically Bangladesh, I came to realize that we needed to add a very strategic person to our team. This would require some thoughtful consideration, along with some prayerful petitions.

Several questions became increasingly prominent the more serious we became about opening NightCare in whatever new country we decided to expand:

How will we do that?

Do we try to find a person currently living in the country where we want to open, who would be interested in starting NightCare, similar to the process I stumbled into when I met Ann, our NightCare Director in Cambodia?

Do we take one of our trained facility managers and move them to the new country, and resource her with money, supplies, language training, and so on?

Do we take someone from America who would be interested in starting NightCare in one of our qualifying countries, move them to that country and equip them, similar to the facility manager option?

The person we needed was someone who could help us get NightCare up and running in new countries. This person would have to travel into multiple countries, and would need to possess some essential skills and abilities. Additionally, this person had to be:

- Morally upstanding, with impeccable character

- Trustworthy with finances

- Adaptable to different cultures

- Able to teach and coach others, according to our NightCare standards, values and daily operations

As Heidi and I started to identify these necessities, we also discussed how to find such an individual. We took a look at our current team to see who, if any, might possess these essential qualities. We concluded that it could be a difficult process to find someone who readily fit these key points, and plug them into a constructive role without some serious ramp-up time, training and investment. At the same time, I began to think about the various leaders we had already developed in Cambodia through our current NightCare operation. I wondered if any of those individuals could pull together all of these ingredients.

That's when I started to think about Ann, our NightCare Director in Cambodia. From the years of working with Ann, I knew her to have impeccable character, morality and integrity. Her financial accounting to our Denver office, on a monthly basis, was virtually error-free, with supporting documents, receipts and bank slips. Since Ann is Irish, she'd already demonstrated her adaptability to various cultures, and she had already been instrumental in launching the four NightCare centers that were operating in Cambodia!

As I floated this idea by Heidi, we immediately began to see some problems that could arise in terms of maintaining the current operational standards for NightCare in Cambodia if we were to promote Ann to a different position. We began to troubleshoot some of the shortfalls and consider possible solutions. Of course, the major question would be if Ann would be willing to move into more of an international role to help us train workers and open NightCare in new countries.

After several weeks of conversations, prayer, reflection and consideration, Ann shifted her role with Saving Moses from being the Director for NightCare in Cambodia, to our International Training Director for NightCare. She would be responsible for opening new NightCare centers in various countries and keeping our current operational standards at our established high level of quality. With this adjustment, we positioned ourselves to start the adventure of opening NightCare in new countries, and I was immensely relieved and excited!

LESSONS LEARNED

IMPERMANENCE

It can be easy to fall into habits and routines, thinking that nothing really changes. And oftentimes, we like to keep things as they are. This has been very true for me with NightCare in terms of going to the same neighborhoods, getting to know the various moms, and being familiar with the surroundings of each center, as well as learning my way through alleyways where one could easily get lost without some consistent travels within those alleys. The truth is that things change. Slums get demolished, people move, and rents on various NightCare centers skyrocket. Change happens!

Working to save babies and toddlers living inside the sex industry has taught me that nothing stays the same for very long. Because of this, I'm continually challenged to stay flexible and adapt. My endgame to protect, nurture and love the babies and toddlers of sex workers doesn't change, but where I do that, and with whom, can vary from season to season.

CREATIVE PROBLEM-SOLVING

If I'm entirely honest with you, I totally enjoy being creative with solving problems. I could say that this is one of my favorite lessons. I like looking at challenges and problems, not as insurmountable or impossible, but rather as opportunities and adventures. And it's possible that because I see problems from the vantage point of opportunities and adventures, perhaps that makes it easier to be creative in addressing them and figuring out solutions.

More than anything, I would say that this lesson has taught me to lean into God for out-of-the-box ideas, and for the ability to see things in new ways. Being prayerful about problems teaches me that the Creator of the Universe has a plethora of answers, solutions and provisions that far exceed my limited human thinking, even when my brain is at optimal function!

CHAPTER 14 - NEW DAY, NEW COUNTRY!

"Sarah, what do you think of this?" I had been corresponding with a friend about the possibility of expanding our NightCare work into different countries, and she sent me a link to a *Washington Post* article. The article described the daily living of a sex worker in a brothel in Bangladesh, along with pictures of a toddler sitting on the bed with her mom who was a sex worker.

The stories in the article, along with the pictures, moved me at an instinctual level, so much that I found myself continually thinking about Bangladesh, and opening NightCare there.

My friend sent me the link in June of 2016, just a couple of months after my snowboarding concussion, but I was keen to make a visit to Bangladesh and investigate the possibilities, despite my brain injury. During the same time period that my friend sent me the link, our Saving Moses team had finalized the evaluation process to identify our top-five countries for opening NightCare; Bangladesh had made that list!

I was increasingly interested in getting over to Bangladesh and was considering a quick visit, in conjunction with our annual July team trip to Cambodia. There was, however, a slight hiccup. At the beginning of July, there was a terrorist attack on a bakery in Dhaka, Bangladesh. Approximately fifty hostages were detained, and ultimately 29 people were killed. When I read about this tragedy, it became obvious to me that doing NightCare in Bangladesh would need to look different than it did in Cambodia. It also alerted me to some possible dangers for Saving Moses, working in this mysterious and intense country.

While these kinds of events can be unsettling, when I considered the big picture and the continuous need for NightCare, I recognized that these types of incidents can happen. But it didn't dissuade me from the possibility of opening NightCare in Bangladesh.

However, I decided to pause visiting Bangladesh in July of 2016, deciding that it would be prudent to let things get more settled in Dhaka, before traveling there to explore the possibilities of opening NightCare.

It is really good that we didn't immediately jump into travel mode because, as I later learned, Bangladesh isn't an easy country in terms of visiting, exploring or transportation. This pause also allowed our team to continue to research and learn more about the brothels, sex industry, transportation and some of the challenges associated with doing humanitarian work in Bangladesh.

While I felt relatively settled, and comfortable with doing NightCare in Cambodia, I came to appreciate that Bangladesh is an entirely different culture. From our research, we learned that there are several legal brothels in Bangladesh, sanctioned by the government. Despite these brothels being recognized by the government, being a sex worker in Bangladesh is illegal.

Additionally, the shame from family members and society in general, associated with being a sex worker in Bangladesh, is drastically more harsh than it is for sex workers in Cambodia. This is due to the history, culture and religion, deeply imbedded in Bangladeshi society. Finally, in Cambodia, sex work is much more evident, widespread and accessible than it is in Bangladesh.

All this extra time for research and preparation before making our first visit to Bangladesh, helped me learn that although there are several legal brothels operating in the nation, getting to those brothels wouldn't be a quick pop-in visit because of the transportation and logistical challenges in this wonderful country.

However, in January of 2017, some of my co-workers and I took a week and visited Bangladesh, which is located along the eastern border of India, and is partially adjacent to Myanmar. Bangladesh gained its independence from India and held its first free elections in 1973. It is currently the eighth most populated country in the world with more than 160 million people, over 90% of which are Muslim. It's also one of the poorest countries in the world with an annual GDP per capita of just over $1,500 in 2017 [1]. We also learned that there are approximately twenty legal brothels in Bangladesh. During our visit in January, we visited three of the twenty brothels and spent the majority of our time at the largest brothel, Daulatdia.

Walking through those brothels was an incredible expedition. We encountered a wide range of reactions to our presence, from joy and friendly exchanges to suspicion and the very real threat of violent aggression. For example, in one of the brothels we visited, with approximately 400 sex workers, I didn't feel safe at all.

We walked into a large closed building, along a narrow and dimly lit hallway, with doorways and open space windows that had vertical jail-like bars instead of curtains. As I looked into each doorway or window, I smiled and tried to make friendly eye-contact. But the longer we walked through the hallways, the more I received hostile looks from the men in the claustrophobic hallway, and sullen stares from the women in each room.

There were more and more men that seemed to be following us; ominous, threatening, louder and more aggressive in tone as they talked to the local Bangladeshi people who were helping us. I became increasingly aware of the tension, and we rapidly decided with our hosts that it would be in our best interest to exit the brothel as quickly as possible. Translation: it was getting more and more dangerous the longer we stayed in that place.

---

[1] https://data.worldbank.org/indicator/ny.gdp.pcap.cd?locations=bd

In contrast, during our visit to a different brothel by the riverside, we had almost the opposite result. It was an outdoor arrangement with fewer sex workers. As we began to walk through the brothel, I could hear someone angrily yelling in the distance. The longer we walked, the louder the yelling became, until I met the woman who was making all the racket. As we approached the hostile yelling, I had a few thoughts about being afraid, and I was a little concerned about what and who we might find.

When I got close to the woman who had been doing all of the yelling, I carefully approached her. When I smiled at her, she gave me a sullen nod. She sized me up and probably concluded that I was a dumb foreigner who was randomly taking a stroll through her neighborhood brothel. She seemed to deem me harmless and naïve.

In only a few minutes, after some brief dialogue with our local Bangladeshi hosts, her edge softened and she became friendlier. She was holding a baby who was sleeping, despite the ruckus his mom had been raising. I motioned to ask if I could hold her baby. She began to smile and soften, delicately passing her baby to me as he continued to sleep. I lovingly held her baby close, and our local hosts explained to her about my interest in starting NightCare, possibly in that brothel.

From that point, all of her anger and hostility melted; she became warm, and even friendly and welcoming. Her countenance softened, her shoulders relaxed, and her voice became gentler. She even allowed us to take her picture with me. In this picture, she is smiling and beautiful, not the angry, combative and hostile sex worker yelling at a neighbor.

No doubt her existence hardens her outlook and interactions. But under her gruff exterior is a kind, tender, warm and congenial woman. I would suspect she likes herself better when she doesn't have to be defensive, protective and contentious, just to eke out a meager existence for herself and her baby. I was grateful to have the opportunity and time to sit with this mom and her baby, and to appreciate who she is beyond her gruff exterior.

The day after we visited the smaller riverside brothel, we went to the largest brothel in Bangladesh, Daulatdia, which was home to anywhere from 1300-1800 sex workers. On the 45-minute drive to the brothel, I found myself getting a little nervous because I didn't know what to expect. My contemplation of the happenings of the preceding day, at the town and riverside brothels, helped me to get my bearings in terms of proper etiquette and friendly interaction in the Bangladeshi culture. But I was nervous because Daulatdia is huge by comparison to the town and riverside brothels. It is also pretty famous in terms of brothel notoriety.

When we arrived at Daulatdia, after some initial pleasantries and introductions to the hosts, we received some basic information about staying together as a group, and we were told that our walking tour would last about 30 minutes. They explained that Daulatdia was a walled and self-contained village, barely tolerated by the neighboring communities. In fact, in recent years, the brothel had been burned down by those communities, who had been protesting this type of work being so close to their homes and families.

We also learned that only in recent years have the women who lived there won some basic legal rights. These include the right to wear shoes (previously a stigma to identify sex workers who might leave their brothel for a brief errand), and the right to have a proper burial, rather than their body being thrown into the nearby river upon death.

All of this was very concerning to me and I felt very serious, and maybe a little nervous, as we began our walk to the walled village. I was deep in thought, absorbing the realities and treading along the littered dirt pathway, but I noticed amongst the trash along the trail a plethora of condom wrappers and used condoms.

Whenever I see such garbage from a brothel, including the leftover rubbish normal for this industry, it's always an initial shock to my system. Then, I am quickly grateful for the protected sex, whenever it happens in a brothel, since the alternative option can be deadly. And I thought to myself, "Welcome to the largest brothel in Bangladesh, Sarah. What else would you expect?"

We squeezed through a barely open doorway, which led into a narrow alleyway, and we were in Daulatdia; close confines, narrow passages, high walls, and guarded observers as we walked along. Thankfully, there was a bit of comic relief as we moved through the first alleyway. I was surprised and curious to see an elderly gentleman, bent over with a wooden box strapped to his back. What immediately caught my attention was a CD strapped to his forehead!

He was friendly and I greeted him with my broken Bengali. I returned his smile and asked our hosts about the CD on his forehead. Was he the local DJ? Our hosts laughed and explained that he was the local ear cleaner. The CD was used to reflect light so he could see into everyone's ears better for a more thorough cleaning. You never know what or who you'll find in a brothel!

I decided to forego the possible ear cleaning in Daulatdia and continued to follow our hosts. Even though we were told that our tour would take about 30 minutes, I tend to go slower and linger at the back of the group, greeting people and trying to soak in the atmosphere, daily living, smells, feelings, people, sights and sounds.

I figure if I'm going to come halfway around the world and go to all the effort and expense to get to this place, after studying it for more than six months, I didn't want to rush the experience in a 30-minute sprint. So I didn't.

At the same time, I endeavored to respect our hosts and remain attentive to places and people who were less friendly. While I was walking through the brothel and greeting various people, I dialed into each woman, trying to be friendly, making eye contact, and hoping to strike up a short conversation. Of course, I always want to know about her children and if she has babies and toddlers.

At one point in our tour, as I kept falling behind everyone else, I noticed a young girl who may have been about 17 years old. Her eyes were particularly sad, and I stopped to greet her and take a few minutes to chat through the interpreter. As I asked her some questions, her eyes began to well up with tears, and I instantly hugged her and tenderly held her as she broke down in my arms.

I found myself crying with her, feeling her despair and later learning about her plight and the hopelessness she felt. She had only been in Daulatdia for a few months, and through the interpreter she explained that she was homesick. I think she felt trapped and despondent, collapsing in my arms at the thought of endless days of such a hellish existence.

I held her for several minutes and we cried together. I lingered by her side for some more time as our translator talked with her and she became more settled. To this day, I still pray for her to be protected by God and directed to a better existence.

Walking through the brothel, I saw the homes where the women work, serving anywhere from four to fifteen clients per night. The women aren't ever allowed to leave the closed village, nor do the neighboring communities welcome sex workers to visit their markets or mingle in their daily social exchanges.

I arrived at one location that seemed safe, where the women appeared free to talk. I asked a group of the sex workers about their children, and I immediately had lots of energetic input! Moms who were lifeless and wooden when talking about their daily existence, suddenly came to life when they talked about their children. They told me how many children they had, the ranges of their ages, about their schooling, hobbies, future hopes and their concerns about what their children are exposed to on any given day.

When I asked the women about what they do with their babies and toddlers while they work, eight out of ten of the women said that their baby or toddler is on the bed with her as she works. Furthermore, they explained that it's not uncommon for a client to finish with the mom and roll over and molest her toddler. Upon asking those moms if they would be interested in having NightCare available for their babies and toddlers, they unanimously and vociferously replied, "YES!"

When we think about women who are in the sex industry, it's helpful to see them as humans and not merely functions. Here's the perspective of Jim, a team traveler to Cambodia, about the moms who are also sex workers:

"Before I became involved in Saving Moses, the world was very black and white to me. There is right and there is wrong. Prostitution was wrong under any circumstance. After going to Cambodia and working with NightCare five times, my perspective changed dramatically. I had a chance to meet the mothers and children. We had a chance to talk to them about their hopes, fears, and dreams. They all wanted the same thing for their children. They wanted their children to grow up, get a good education, and be successful. I learned that mothers are the same regardless of ethnicity, vocation, or faith. The love a mother has for her children is no different in the sex districts of Cambodia than mothers in the suburbs of Denver. We look at sex workers in the United States and we get visuals of Las Vegas with a certain amount of glamour. In many nations across the world, women get into the sex industry because their mothers and grandmothers were in the business. It is simply a way to squeak out a living. Unfortunately, the work is hard and dangerous with little pay. Most of the mothers I met were just trying to make a living...Nothing about it is glamourous. No designer clothes or limousines. Just life as they have always known it."

And so began my earnest work to open a NightCare center where we could take care of the babies and toddlers of the moms working in Daulatdia. That first visit to Bangladesh was in January of 2017, and I came home with an almost overwhelming passion and laser-sharp focus to get NightCare up and running near Daulatdia as quickly as possible. To turn my dream into a reality, our team doubled down in their efforts and hammered out a boatload of logistics to establish NightCare for the babies and toddlers of the sex workers in Daulatdia.

In the middle of July, our key people in Cambodia, Ann and Narith, went with me to Daulatdia. We worked with a local organization that was already providing assistance to sex workers there. In partnership with this organization, we were able to sort out some critical priorities, such as a child protection policy, care standards, reporting and oversight requirements, along with financial accountability. With these conversations and arrangements in place, we had everything organized to move forward with opening NightCare within a few short months. Needless to say, I was ecstatic!

At the same time, I was also preparing myself to settle in for a long haul to earn our place and win the trust of those moms by providing NightCare. I vividly remembered the monumental task we had faced in Cambodia to earn the trust of the moms and I expected the same challenges in Bangladesh. I was coaching my own mental game, telling myself to be patient and not expect a jubilant welcome or acceptance from these moms, given my track record in Cambodia. "Go slowly. Be dependable. Stay steady. Be trustworthy." I was hopeful that we'd see possibly six babies and toddlers from the outset and then build from there. But I was wrong.

I was almost shocked by the number of babies in NightCare! During the first four months of operation, we averaged no less than 20 babies and toddlers every night. And since then, we've run approximately 30 babies and toddlers each night. This is extremely exciting for me, just for the sheer numbers.

Furthermore, when I inquired about the total number of babies and toddlers in Daulatdia, I learned that there are about 120 children in our target age-range, and with our average of 30 babies nightly, this means that we're reaching almost 25% of the whole group in less than a year of being in existence! I appreciate that we're not at 100% yet, but from time to time, it's helpful to celebrate some victories and progress!

While we have good reason to celebrate establishing NightCare in Daulatdia with such wonderful attendance numbers, let me tell you about a little girl who attends our NightCare every night. Saba is a three-year-old girl whose mom is a sex worker in Daulatdia. Saba was born in Daulatdia and has only known what it is like to live in a brothel.

As dangerous as it was, as her mom earned a living every night with a virtual revolving door of clients, Saba either stayed on the bed with her mom as she worked, or she stayed tucked into a corner of the same room. Saba's mom was desperate to find an alternative place that was safe for her daughter to stay while she worked, but there was nothing, until we started NightCare.

Saba is now one of the 30 babies and toddlers who attend NightCare, and it's making a world of difference in her life. After several months in NightCare, she is more settled and less disobedient. She exhibits more confidence than before NightCare, and she's even starting to learn the beginnings of the alphabet, along with shapes and colors. While NightCare may seem simple, it makes a life-changing difference for each baby and toddler who attends.

Along with the progress that we've made with opening NightCare in Daulatdia, I'm also deeply compelled by the opportunities for NightCare in other parts of Bangladesh. For example, during my first visit to Bangladesh, I also had the privilege of meeting a network of "floating" sex workers in Dhaka. When I was first presented with the opportunity to meet with this network, I didn't really understand the term "floating sex worker."

Thankfully, everyone was very patient with me and explained that there aren't any official brothels in Dhaka, a city with more than 20 million people. In such a large city, it's helpful to consider some critical contributing factors to the lives of these floating sex workers, which include income and education. Consider these statistics:

- GDP: Bangladesh - 177th out of 229 in the world at $4,200; US - 19th with $59,500 [1]

- Female literacy rates for all ages - 133rd out of 160 countries at 58.5% [2]

- 56% literacy rate among adult females [3]

---

[1] https://www.cia.gov/Library/publications/the-world-factbook/rankorder/2004rank.html

[2] http://world.bymap.org/LiteracyRatesFemales.html

[3] https://data.unicef.org/topic/education/literacy/

Because of these factors and many others, there is an underground industry of floating sex workers in Dhaka. They are called "floaters" since they don't work in an official brothel, but rather "float" on the streets to acquire clients and earn a living. I can appreciate that this would seem rather strange to the average American mindset. But in this overpopulated city with such extreme poverty, transient populations, high unemployment, and low education, sex working can generate a much-needed income, though women in the sex industry are extremely shamed in that culture for religious and social reasons.

As such, these floating sex workers have been ostracized and severely maligned. With such marginalization, they have banded together to form a network, or a union of sorts. As members of the network, the women are granted access to various services and legal representation, and the network aims to improve the lives of its members.

There are approximately 15,000 registered floaters in the network and the leaders from this network explained to me that for every registered member, there are at least five unregistered. If you run the numbers, that would mean that there are at least 90,000 floating sex workers in Dhaka. I can appreciate that many residents of Dhaka might take issue with me on such a high number, but I would argue that in a city of more than 20 million people, with such high poverty, illiteracy and unemployment, I can't imagine how there could be less than .5% sex workers in Dhaka.

But here's the real rub for these floating sex workers: there is absolutely no care, protection or steady resources for their babies and toddlers. So, imagine my horror when a floater told me how she left her 14-month-old son in what she thought was a safe place while she was working on the streets; when she returned to collect him, he was missing, and she never found him again.

Another floater put a tangle of twine in my hand, explaining in Bengali how she ties it around her toddler's ankle or wrist. Then she ties the other end to an object near her, or even around her own ankle, as she works so she doesn't lose her child. This is the day-to-day reality of a floating sex worker in Dhaka. Needless to say, I am deeply distressed by what I've learned, and we are on the cusp of opening NightCare for the babies and toddlers of those floaters.

As I step back and think about what's been accomplished with NightCare in just a few years, I'm astounded by what we've been able to do. And yet, I am also fiercely committed to doing more! I have to be careful to regulate myself and not push beyond what is manageable and healthy, while pressing forward to protect and look after more and more precious babies and toddlers!

LESSONS LEARNED

LOVE TRUMPS FEAR

Being involved in the sex industry in developing countries can be scary; full stop. There are lots of legitimate reasons to be afraid, or at the minimum, careful. The pillars of this industry are intimidation, vulnerability, domination and survival. And, in my opinion, it capitalizes on what is worst in the human race, fear being a universal and timeless torment. After walking through brothels and interacting with people who breathe fear every second like it is oxygen, one can choose to swallow this poison or make a different decision.

1 John 4:18 says that perfect love casts out fear. In my thinking, the antidote for fear is love. And I've seen this antidote make fear tuck its tail and scurry to find another victim when I choose to express genuine love. This lesson isn't merely for brothels and sex workers; it is applicable in all of our lives regardless of where we live, our age, economic security, education, etc. Never forget that perfect love casts out fear!

SHOW UP

In our very busy and demanding life, it's easy to find distractions and justifications for being absent, or even disinterested. Such rationalizations are very helpful when we feel awkward, insecure, inadequate or downright stupid. When I walk through brothels, I often feel like a fish out of water - like I don't belong and that I'm an interloper. But I still show up because I love sincerely and genuinely.

Sometimes the best way to express genuine love is simply showing up and being present. To be present can mean that we listen, fix our attention and eyes on someone, or even just walk alongside another person. It's important to show up; full stop.

CHAPTER 15 - WHAT'S NEXT?

As we finish looking at the amazing journey my team and I have taken to turn NightCare from a dream into a magnificent reality, I want to make you aware of an opportunity that is available to you, at the time this book is being written. It is a unique opportunity and probably something you have never considered. For several years now, we have taken a relatively small team to Cambodia to help us with NightCare for a week, and it has been a wonderful experience for many travelers who have come with us. In fact, more than half of our first-time travelers sign up to do another trip in a succeeding year. We even have some team members who have been on five or more trips over the years.

Our team trips generally follow a simple daily schedule; team devotions in the morning, breakfast and a short jaunt to the assigned center. At the centers, over the course of the week a team will do facility upgrades by cleaning, repairing simple things, painting and providing general upkeep. Additionally, each team gets to meet and interview a different mom each day. Each mom is a sex worker who regularly brings her baby to NightCare. These interviews provide powerful insights into how a mom endeavors to provide for, and look after, her baby.

After the interview, the team gets lunch and has a little bit of down time in the afternoon before heading out to their NightCare center to get ready to welcome the babies and toddlers who will be arriving throughout the evening. After spending a few hours playing with the kids, helping with mealtime, consoling upset toddlers, cleaning spills, joining circle time with songs, counting, reciting ABC's and a story, the team heads out for dinner and the NightCare nannies put all of the babies and toddlers down to sleep for the night. In the morning, the moms collect their baby or toddler and take them home with them for the day.

Here are a few insights from some of the team members who have joined our trip to experience NightCare in Cambodia. To facilitate some feedback, I interviewed a few of our travelers with specific questions. You will see their answers below.

Describe your time in the NightCare center for one evening.

"NightCare is really similar to any type of Western daycare center. Moms drop their babies off, often looking relieved to get a short break from the chaos of trying to care for a baby or toddler. Toddlers run in with exuberance, knowing the routine of the night: bath time, clean clothes, mealtime, playtime, circle time with singing and lessons, snack time, and then bedtime. It's loud and a bit crazy at times, but the joy of children being children is a beautiful sight to witness. They're not perfect angels inside of the NightCare walls - they carry the habits of their home with them: violence, frustration, survival mentality, desperation for attention - but the NightCare staff gently steers them to safety, appropriate behaviors, and kind words. It's a picture of patience, slowly but surely working on behavioral outputs through genuine love and care." • Julie

"The evening routine at NightCare is unadulterated goodness. It's just pure, wholehearted, Jesus-with-skin-on goodness. The babies and toddlers are experiencing heaven on earth compared to the hell of their normal surroundings." • Emily

"The kids come in, some running and others crying as they depart from their mom for the night. They get a bath and clean pjs before being released to play. Pretty soon chaos ensues as multiple children are running, screaming and laughing as babies and toddlers tend to do. I see these kids having fun without a care in the world and it brings me such joy. I know the stories of these kids, I have seen where they live, I know what they already have lived through, and yet they are happy in spite of the circumstances. Then comes circle time and singing songs and the occasional chicken dance if the kids are still super hyper. Finally, it's bedtime as they all march upstairs and wave or hug goodnight to their new friends. That is when my heart melts, when I leave my kids for the night knowing they are safe and cared for. Knowing what could wait for them without NightCare, it is encouraging to depart knowing they are safe and loved." • Morgan

"As a man working in NightCare, I was very sensitive to what the children may think of me. First of all, I am older, white, and completely gray. Most of them have not seen people like me very often in their neighborhoods. I did not know what experiences they have had with men and generally they looked at me with great caution. After a couple of days of gaining their trust, most finally warmed up to me to play. It became obvious to me that they are looking for men that they can trust and feel safe around. I felt that I could show them the love of God and hopefully plant the seed in their young lives that all men are not bad or abusive. Perhaps their image of God can be positive through their interaction with me." • Jim

What was singularly the most powerful experience for you from joining the NightCare work?

"I have heard so many horror stories at this point about what these people and specifically the kids go through. At times I can find myself calloused to those stories as they happen often in this world. But I can't block those stories when it happens to a child. To hear this child was beaten, this child was sexually abused, this child was sold, I can't be calloused to *those stories. It's in those moments I see exactly why NightCare exists and why it should. NightCare takes these stories that should end in disaster and turns them into success stories. It takes the broken, abused child and shows them what love is and gives them a chance to be whole. NightCare is changing a generation from broken and abused to loved. I join with NightCare because it is the only chance some of these babies would ever get to feel love."* • Morgan

"For me, the importance of hope and resources to grow into who you want to be really stood out to me. Many of these moms were my age and many had children much earlier. These moms had been through things that I couldn't even imagine myself going through at ages much earlier than anyone ever should. It really demonstrated to me just the pure luck that I have that I was born into the situation that I was born into. Meeting with the moms and bonding with the other young women who worked at the NightCare center really showed me how dramatic the differences in our situations can be, and the importance of having that encouragement around us to provide us the opportunity to be our best selves. For these moms, NightCare is that opportunity. If we can alleviate one stress in their already intense daily routine, then that opens the door just a bit for possibilities and hope to enter into their lives. It isn't about where we are now, and not even where we could be, but where we are with Jesus and where we are with others. Compassion and encouragement were the two main themes that I could take away from my experience there. We never know what others are dealing with, the mountains they are climbing or the decisions they are faced with, but kindness and encouragement can really help those around us make it another day." • Caitlyn

Reading these interviews encourages me to keep going and not be settled or content with what we have achieved so far. I say this because of a question I was recently asked. "Would you please open NightCare for my toddler? I have no place where I can leave him while I work and where he will be safe." This was one of many similar pleas from moms who are floating sex workers in Bangladesh.

I keep seeing one of the moms, who stands out in my memory. She has tender eyes, a winsome smile and a gentle demeanor. She was in a group of the floating sex workers, all of them telling me about their daily living, the very real and dangerous risks for their toddlers and babies, along with various tragedies and traumas they had suffered.

This mom with tender eyes stayed alongside me, after I had listened to everyone. We walked about half a mile to a possible location for NightCare, where there were rooms available for rent. She held my hand and snuggled close to me, such that I'll never forget meeting her.

As we toured the possible NightCare location, I was certain to ask her opinion and input; if it would be a good space and place for her toddler and if the other floaters would like it too. Was it a good location with relatively easy access for the floating sex workers? Did it seem safe to her? Would she be comfortable leaving her toddler there with proper care and supervision? She mostly looked at me and smiled with a mix of hope and sadness in her eyes.

It's these moments that continually cling to me. They never stop challenging and changing me. It's not so much that they haunt me, as much as they drill determination, and anchor resolve, deep in my soul to genuinely love the babies and toddlers of sex workers in the developing world. I find myself a walking contradiction. In one sense, I'm altogether thrilled about what's been accomplished in such a short time, and in another sense, I'm heartbroken that we aren't moving faster and doing more.

I'm also encouraged that we now have a full-time International NightCare Training Manager, and she is both excited and effective with improving the quality of our care, as well as opening new centers in several countries.

There are approximately twenty brothels in Bangladesh and no less than 200,000 sex workers in this country [1]. They are housed in brothels,

---

[1] https://www.researchgate.net/publication/299506841_Economics_of_Sex_Work_in_Bangladesh

floating on the streets and working in hotels. We are actively working to expand NightCare in Bangladesh. While I'd like to provide NightCare for all of these needs (brothels, floaters and hotel sex workers), right now we are endeavoring to be strategic and triage what's most urgent and least available. And many times, we are only able to fully prioritize what's most urgent and least available by being in the country several times.

At this time, we have identified three more countries in the developing world context where NightCare is desperately needed. As I've described throughout these chapters, India is a country with an urgent need for NightCare and that need is growing every year. At present, India has about 1.3 billion people [1], and demographic studies say that its population could exceed China's by 2025 [2]. This means that there are more than 2 million sex workers in India and over 275,000 brothels. There is no shortage of red-light districts scattered throughout this country.

Furthermore, off the east coast of India is the island of Sri Lanka. This is another country we have identified to expand NightCare. Although Sri Lanka doesn't have the vast population that India has, there is a huge number of sex workers there, approximately 50,000 [3]. In addition to the large number of sex workers, there is also extreme poverty, poor education, unemployment and vulnerability for females. These are all factors that work together to position Sri Lanka to be in our top-five countries for expanding NightCare. We have also learned that Sri Lanka is known as the "pedophile's paradise" [4] - all the more reason to open NightCare there!

---

[1] https://www.cia.gov/library/publications/the-world-factbook/geos/in.html

[2] https://www.hindustantimes.com/india-news/india-s-population-growth-rate-is-overestimated-says-study/story-WhmIANZ4ktoVKbkmHaEkwL.html

[3] http://factsanddetails.com/india/People_and_Life/sub7_3h/entry-4190.html

[4] www.gvnet.com/childprostitution/SriLanka.htm

In addition to Sri Lanka, we have identified a significant need for NightCare in the Philippines, where there are 500,000 sex workers [1] and at least half a dozen red-light districts. In one of those red-light districts there are more than 10,000 sex workers, and there is an abundance of evidence to support the need for NightCare in this country [2].

The last country we want to increase our NightCare presence in is the country where we first began, Cambodia.

We currently have five NightCare centers working six nights a week in Cambodia. I'm extremely happy about what we have accomplished in Phnom Penh, and I want to do more. There are no reliable numbers pertaining to the quantity of sex workers in Cambodia, but some sources say there are 35,000 sex workers [3]. Other sources say there are more than 100,000 sex workers [4]. Such a wide range for this number is entirely normal considering the industry being measured isn't a highly accepted or admired profession.

In addition to opening more NightCare centers in Phnom Penh, I'm also super keen to open NightCare in Siem Reap, a city where more than 2 million tourists travel every year to see the archaeological ruins of Angkor Wat [5]. It's a well-known fact that with such high numbers of tourists, there

---

[1] https://web.archive.org/web/20131116040537/http://globaldiscussion.net/topic/1442-countries-with-the-most-prostitutes

[2] https://www.smh.com.au/world/philippines-divided-over-us-return-to-subic-bay-20121119-29m4m.html

[3] http://www.aidsinfoonline.org/gam/stock/shared/dv/Data_2018_7_22_636678151733621264.htm

[4] https://www.news.com.au/lifestyle/real-life/news-life/shocking-reality-of-cambodias-child-sex-workers/news-story/ecfdb242d5e3ad35a2d6d074852f0744

[5] https://www.phnompenhpost.com/business/ticket-revenue-angkor-wat-jumps-72- percent-after-price-hike

is no shortage of opportunities for sex workers to earn a living within the tourism industry. This means there is also a desperate need for NightCare centers in Siem Reap for the babies and toddlers of those sex workers. While it might seem to be relatively easy to open NightCare centers in Siem Reap because we are already established in Phnom Penh, the truth is that there are significant and diverse challenges that are unique to Siem Reap.

And ultimately, in the simplest terms, it is difficult to open a NightCare center anywhere; full stop. Hopefully, this book has informed you of some of the challenges that accompany opening and sustaining NightCare centers and malnutrition clinics. I also want to encourage you that anything that's worth doing is usually difficult and challenging. As I said, if it were easy, it would have already been done.

In this chapter, when I share about what's next, attempting to communicate with numbers the quantity of sex workers in various countries, I want to put something in front of you for consideration. The numbers that I've listed for sex workers in the Philippines, India, Cambodia, Sri Lanka and Bangladesh are most likely conservative estimates. I think these numbers are on the small side for several reasons:

The industry isn't glamorous, so most sex workers don't line up to be identified as such, let alone counted

In many of these countries, prostitution is illegal, so there are strong legal deterrents to being identified as a sex worker

The sex industry is an ever-changing business, adapting to neighborhood pressures, economic realities, drug culture influences, HIV complications, along with a host of other factors and influences

These kinds of things make it difficult to get concrete and verifiable numbers, and the industry evolves to match the demands. But here's the important take-away from all of these numbers, statistics and analysis: Prostitution is giving sex in exchange for money, and sex is the action that can and often does create a baby. So it's not uncommon for a sex worker to have several babies, given her line of profession. And each of these babies didn't ask to be born into his or her mother's profession, nor are they able to protect or advocate for themselves. This reinforces the fact that the need for NightCare centers is extremely significant.

I don't think I could frame the need for NightCare more powerfully than to finish with the story of one of our babies. The first time I met Arun, he was about two years old, and to say that he was a wild child would be the understatement of the century. Arun was pretty much out of control and when he came to NightCare, which had only recently opened, I could sense the NightCare nannies getting a little tense. It didn't take me long to appreciate their stress.

Arun ran around the room, scooped up toys, threw stuff, kicked toys, pushed the other kids and was quite defiant with the NightCare nannies. I was helping to lead one of our team trips, and I wanted to be on the front lines to support our nannies at our newest center. Because it was a team trip, I had several team members with me at the center. One member was Bill, a father in his mid-50s, entirely familiar with the rough and tumble nature of toddler boys. Arun took a liking to Bill, and I learned why over the next few days.

One of the nannies at this center told me that Arun came from a very abusive home. While his mom was a sex worker and had other children, the various boyfriends and men who streamed through Arun's life were horrible. The nanny told me of a time recently, when Arun showed up to NightCare with welts on his legs and arms.

When the nanny asked Arun's mom about his welts, she abruptly explained that she'd briefly left Arun with a boyfriend so that she could go grocery shopping. When she returned, Arun had been lashed with electric cords, leaving the welts that were evident.

The first evening that Bill and I showed up at NightCare, Arun was very elusive and cagey with Bill. And Bill was amazing. He seemed to dial into Arun and have a calming effect on him. Over the course of the next five days, Arun changed and became more settled, compliant and I could see that he deeply valued the opportunity to be around Bill, a safe male figure who was firm and loving.

If you fast forward, Arun has been consistently coming to the same NightCare for almost three years. He's one of the leader kids in his NightCare center and sets the tone for both obedience and excellence. He's a classic rough and tumble little boy who also expresses self-control, respect, gratitude and even a degree of settled contentment. The nannies value his leadership and concurrently recognize that he's an ongoing miracle.

It has been nothing less than my extreme privilege to watch Arun over the years - to see him enter NightCare with fear, abuse, pain and dysfunction and watch him transform through the tender, gentle and faithful expression of genuine love. Would that we could open hundreds of NightCare centers to facilitate, to communicate and to express genuine love!

CONCLUDING THOUGHTS

As I come to the end of writing this book, in my heart I feel like I'm just getting warmed up, and maybe I've hardly started. At the same time, writing this book has helped me appreciate just how much has been accomplished in a very short amount of time. Such accomplishments are contrasted with the immensity of what is needed. It has been a grand adventure to be sure, and I'm eager to write the sequel to this book as time unfolds and we become increasingly more effective and expansive.

On this grand adventure so far, our work with malnutrition in Africa has been abundantly rewarding. It's rewarding to see the change in data, with a significantly decreased number of deaths and babies withdrawn from our clinics before getting healthy and being released. It's also rewarding to follow up with babies who turn into toddlers and then become vibrant and thriving children with a hopeful future. It is very fulfilling to see the effects of our consistent malnutrition commitment. And I know there's more to be done on this front!

Also, on this grand adventure, we are only just beginning to explore the possibilities with NightCare in developing countries. A massive difference can be made in the worldview of babies and toddlers when genuine love is part of their daily living as they attend our NightCare centers. The critical survival needs of babies and toddlers are not only related to proper nutrition, food intake and clean water. Each baby and toddler needs to experience genuine love in these formative years so their worldview can be constructive and functional, rather than transactional and dysfunctional.

The future starts with babies and toddlers, today. The life of each baby and toddler whom we serve is hanging by a thread, and it is our supreme honor and passion to step into their precarious existence, tie a knot in the thread and facilitate a more secure and certain future!

Where the need is most urgent and the care is least available, we are committed to providing genuine love, care and resources for babies and toddlers throughout the world!

May God bless us with discomfort at easy answers, half-truths, and superficial relationships, so that we may live deep within our hearts.

May God bless us with anger at injustice, oppression, and exploitation of people, so that we may work for justice, freedom and peace.

May God bless us with tears to shed for those who suffer from pain, rejection, starvation and war, so that we may reach out our hands to comfort them and turn their pain into joy.

And may God bless us with enough foolishness to believe that we can make a difference in this world, so that we can do what others claim cannot be done. [1]

---

[1] http://epistle.us/inspiration/franciscanbenediction.html

ENDORSEMENTS

"This book is guaranteed to challenge you. Think for a moment if one of these little ones were your child. Would you not do anything to relieve the pain and provide a better life? That is exactly what Sarah has done for 10 years. Allow this book and the stories of these precious little ones to do something to make a difference in someone else's life who is in need."

David L. Meyer, *CEO of Hand of Hope*

Sarah is the real deal! She has written an inspiring book, "Hanging by a Thread: The Saving Moses Journey", which details the founding of the non-profit she started, Saving Moses. Her genuine love for people and her tenacity in reaching those that have been the most marginalized will challenge and encourage every reader to truly begin to love 'the least of these.' Enjoy the book, and then get one for a friend!

Holly Wagner, *Pastor of Oasis Church, Author of "Find Your Brave," Founder of She Rises*

From the first time I became aware of Sarah Bowling's ministry assignment, Saving Moses, I was deeply touched! I love and admire Sarah's proactiveness and tenacity. In 1 Corinthians 13:13, we find that "...faith, hope, love, abide these three but the greatest of these is love." Sarah and her team intentionally live this verse as they save the lives and destinies of countless babies. As you read, "Hanging by a Thread", you will not only be touched but you will be changed and invited to take action...we can all do something!

Dr. Patricia King, *Author, Television Host, Minister*

www.patriciaking.com

In "Hanging by a Thread: The Saving Moses Journey", Sarah descriptively brings us along with her into some of the seediest back alleys of darkness. Her redemptive stories inspire us with reminders of how God's love can shine hope and light into human hearts full of despair. Thank you, Sarah for writing a book that will stir every reader towards courage and compassion.

Jonathan Shibley, *President of Global Advance*

Sarah Bowling has a passion to live out the life-changing truth of being a servant of Christ, especially in outreaches to the poor. She knows it is not in our comfort zones where God uses us most. Sarah has taken the mantle to go on a "great adventure with God," and she shows us transformational change among malnourished children in Africa and through a remarkable night care ministry to babies of women trapped in the sex trades. Her travels, and her life, reveal what it means to make a kingdom difference here on earth!

James Robison, *President of LIFE Outreach International, Fort Worth, Texas*

In "Hanging by a Thread" Sarah Bowling takes us into some of the darkest corners of the world and shines a light on the poignant vulnerability of the least of these. For the stories it tells, for the love it exhibits, and for the hope it instills, Hanging by a Thread is a book worth reading.

Brian Zahnd, *Lead pastor of Word of Life Church in St. Joseph, Missouri and author of "Postcards From Babylon"*

There is a huge difference between a good idea and an idea to do good. Sarah Bowling had a good idea about how to do good to those who need it most. Her newest book, "Hanging By A Thread," not only documents *the beginning of her precious ministry; it also lights the way forward for all those with the great idea of doing good to God's precious ones.*

Mark Rutland, *Founder of Global Servants & President of Oral Roberts University*

"Hanging by a Thread" is a beautiful and touching story of one woman's response to the plight of the most vulnerable in our world. With the wisdom and earnestness of a caring pastor, Sarah invites us into her journey of hope, possibilities, and grand adventures with God.

Nathan Foster, *Director of Community Life, Renovaré, author of "The Making of an Ordinary Saint"*

2009 - Sarah Bowling pictured with babies, Sarah and Ruth, one year after finding them abandoned in a field. Meeting them and hearing their story led to the beginning of Saving Moses.

2010 - Sarah traveled to Angola where thousands of babies were dying from Severe Acute Malnutrition (SAM). On this trip, she met Belito (pictured here), one of the babies suffering from SAM.

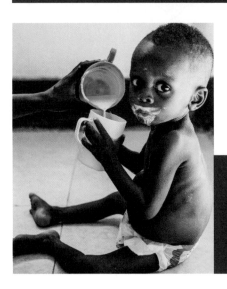

2010 - Saving Moses started the Angola therapeutic milk program for babies suffering from SAM.

2011- Sarah met Anne, who was instrumental in opening and running the first Saving Moses NightCare Centers.

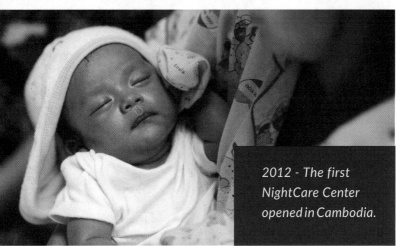

2012 - The first NightCare Center opened in Cambodia.

2014 - Saving Moses took the first official team trip to Cambodia.

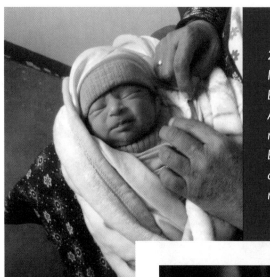

2015- The Birth and Infant Aid program began in Central Asia providing midwives, safe birthing education, and pre and post-natal vaccinations.

2015- The Saving Moses team returned to Angola and visited Belito, who was five, healthy, and in school.

2017- Sarah visited Bangladesh and opened a new NightCare Center.

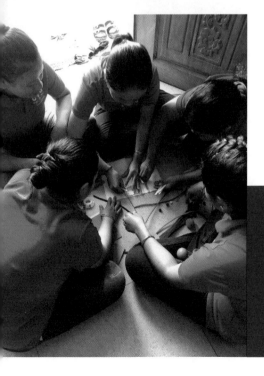

2018- Staff training in Cambodia for five NightCare Centers operating in Cambodia.